the nature of
ANTHROPOLOGY

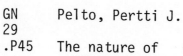
GN
29
.P45

Pelto, Pertti J.

The nature of
anthropology

DATE DUE			

the nature of

ANTHROPOLOGY

Pertti J. Pelto

Department of Anthropology
University of Minnesota

George D. Spindler, *Consultant*

Department of Anthropology
Stanford University

CHARLES E. MERRILL BOOKS, INC., Columbus, Ohio

To Pat, Gina, Joshua, and Dunja,
Who all had a hand in this work

Printed in the United States of America

Preface

The rapid explosion of knowledge makes it essential that *The Nature of Anthropology* be presented in a most revealing manner for those who seek intelligent understandings about the discipline of anthropology and its relationships to modern technological and humanistic endeavors.

The Nature of Anthropology is designed to develop basic knowledge about anthropology's unique organizational structure, its scope, and its character as a discipline. Recognizing the need for greater insight into this unusual, dramatic and sometimes puzzling field of study, specific information about the backgrounds, the methods, the tools, and critical viewpoints that are fundamentally relevant have been presented.

Throughout this volume the physical and cultural aspects of man and his works unfold into a logical, manageable system that can be easily understood with deeper appreciation and decided benefit to the reader and his associates in the years ahead.

Charles E. Merrill Books, Inc.

Foreword

Anthropology, together with the other social sciences, is today confronted with three fundamental challenges, for which the individual scholar must form his own answers.

The first of these challenges arises from increasing public pressures on scientists to find solutions to the great range of social problems besetting modern man. In earlier times, anthropologists and other social scientists were seldom consulted by governments and little heeded by the general public. They found it easy to pursue their research interests without pressure to produce immediate results or the need to prove the practicality of their speculations, however much they may have believed in the usefulness of their efforts. It is relevant that in earlier years social scientists received very little public financial support.

In recent times, though, political leaders and the educated public increasingly have turned to the scientific community for solutions to social problems; state and national governments have made large grants for social research; and social scientists have been drawn into extensive discussion of ways to combat social disorganization, reduce international tensions, and generally minister to the ills of mankind. Anthropologists have had an important share in these developments, particularly as public attention has shifted toward social change among peoples of the non-Western world.

Since man has the habit of discussing his social problems with vehemence and conviction, it is becoming difficult for the social or behavioral scientist—who is a mere mortal—to maintain anything like the ethical neutrality and impartiality generally thought necessary to successful scientific research. Some meet this problem by maintaining two identities. When acting as research scientists they strive to remain ethically neutral and objective, simply trying to find out "the facts." On other occasions, though, they take on the identity of "informed private citizens," who go beyond the impartial

facts to engage in spirited discussion about how scientific information is to be used for the public welfare. The social scientist who
prefers to remain aloof from public discussion, or who chooses to
pursue research that is deemed "impractical" or "too theoretical"
by the government or by the lay public may have difficulty in
obtaining financial support for his work.

The second major challenge to anthropology is more technical.
Our experiences with research in all branches of the social sciences
tell us that the "facts" we seek are extremely elusive. For the greater
part of the nineteenth century anthropologists believed and taught
a series of ideas about the evolution of human culture which they
felt to be self-evident truths. Anthropologists of the twentieth
century for a long time maintained ideas and theories that were
quite in contradiction to those earlier views. And today anthropologists still have wide differences of opinion on these same issues.
The great debates in anthropological theory have not been resolved.

From an examination of the changes in fashions of anthropological thought over the past decades, it becomes clear that we
are still far from establishing the standards of evidence and research
methods that would put the "science of man" on a solid footing.
It is well to remember that progress in the biological and physical
sciences, too, was relatively slow until men developed research
methods that could be duplicated and re-evaluated by other researchers; success came to the physical scientists by way of highly
controlled laboratory research.

But such highly controlled laboratory methods are not possible
in the study of human behavior. Anthropologists and their fellow
social scientists are therefore faced with enormous problems in their
search for precision of description and analysis in studies that in
large part must be made in real life rather than in the laboratory.

Finally, anthropologists together with all scholars are confronted with the enormity of today's "information revolution." In
many fields of study the total mass of scientific information doubles
every few years. New books are published in great profusion, and
many new scientific journals have been established to accommodate
new areas of specialized knowledge. Scholars who would keep up
with the latest developments in their special fields must spend
ever increasing amounts of time studying the products of new
research.

Part of the problem of information organization and storage is
handled by computerized facilities and other highly technical information systems, which sometimes gives the scholar a feeling of

alienation from his own research materials. Information punched onto IBM cards somehow seems more remote and unreal than words and pictures in the books we search out in the dusty stacks of libraries.

Anthropologists traditionally have maintained a sturdy suspicion of complex research "gadgets" and computerized information processing. But the volume of information and the problems of gaining scientific precision in research now demand that anthropologists turn to the more technologically advanced sciences for methods of processing and analyzing information.

Among the sciences, then, anthropology can be regarded as in some ways analogous to a "developing nation," receiving aid from the more technologically advanced sciences, while resisting and resenting the violence done to established traditions. Continuing this analogy, we can also say that anthropologists are selective in their acceptance of technological innovations, and they sometimes develop ways of using scientific research tools that were not intended by the original inventors.

Given the great pace of change in the sciences, and the varieties of opinion and theory in the social sciences particularly, it will hardly come as a surprise if my brief description in this book does not accord with the picture many others might present of the anthropological discipline. Each of us has his own version of the contours of his chosen field of study. My primary task will have been accomplished if this short account spurs at least some readers to search out more of the exciting materials of anthropology.

Pertti J. Pelto
Minneapolis, 1966

Contents

the nature of
ANTHROPOLOGY

chapter one

The Study of Man

By the beginning of the twentieth century the scholars who interested themselves in the unusual, dramatic, and puzzling aspects of man's history were known as anthropologists. They were the men who were searching for man's most remote ancestors; for Homer's Troy; for the original home of the American Indian; for the relationship between bright sunlight and skin color; for the origin of the wheel, safety pins, and pottery. They wanted to know "how modern man got that way": why some people are ruled by a king, some by old men, others by warriors, and none by women; why some peoples pass on property in the male line, others in the female line, still others equally to heirs of both sexes; why some people fall sick and die when they think they are bewitched, and others laugh at the idea. They sought for the universals in human biology and in human conduct. They proved that men of different continents and regions were physically much more alike than they were different. They discovered many parallels in human customs, some of which could be explained by historical contact. In other words, anthropology had become the science of human similarities and differences.[1]

The broadest and ·boldest definition of anthropology states simply that "anthropology is the study of man and his works." And, in fact, only that very broad definition can include all the varied field studies, theoretical interests, and teaching areas of people who call themselves anthropologists. Under the title "Anthropology" in the course catalogues of major universities, we

[1] Clyde Kluckhohn, *Mirror for Man* (New York: McGraw-Hill Book Co., Inc., 1949), p. 2.

notice first that this field of study is usually divided into two main branches—physical anthropology and cultural (or social) anthropology. Most anthropology departments offer two separate introductory courses corresponding to these two aspects of the study of man.

PHYSICAL ANTHROPOLOGY

Ever since the great Swedish naturalist Linnaeus published his monumental classification of plants and animals in the eighteenth century, man has been listed among the animals, and the study of man has been regarded as a branch of natural science. An important aspect of biological anthropology is the examination of the many-sided evidence for the evolution of man from "lower" forms of animal life. Therefore, introductory courses in physical anthropology often begin with materials on the comparative anatomy of *Homo sapiens* and his nearest "cousins," the apes and monkeys, all fellow members of the order of mammals called *Primates*. Then they may study the fossil evidence of human evolution in the form of fossilized bones of Neandertal Man, Java Man and a great number of other fragments from men and ape-men that lived hundreds of thousands of years ago. Interest in man's biological relationships with the other primates also leads to a comparative study of the social behavior of subhuman primates, such as the gorillas, chimpanzees, and baboons.

The variations among different physical populations of *Homo sapiens*, commonly divided into Mongoloid, Negroid, Caucasoid and several smaller racial stocks, are another major concern of the physical anthropologists. Recent developments in the science of genetics have changed the study of racial classifications from a dull cataloguing of obvious traits (color of skin, eye color, head shape, height, etc.) into an exciting search for patterns in the genetic inheritance of blood types, resistance to particular diseases, and examination of biological adaptation to different world climates.

In addition to these two relatively well-known lines of interest, physical anthropology has become increasingly concerned with the study of human growth and constitution, relationships of nutrition to body build, and a number of other physiological problems that bring anthropology into close contact with the special fields of anatomy, radiobiology, serology, physiology, and general medicine.

CULTURAL (SOCIAL) ANTHROPOLOGY

The distinctive feature that makes man so different from other animals is that the human pattern of life is based on "culture,"— socially learned patterns of behavior, based on symbolic processes. Other animals may have some rudiments of culture, but for man *all* behavior is pervasively cultural. The several different facets of human culture (culture history, language, social structures, personality, etc.) give rise to a series of subfields that may be grouped in a variety of ways in the teaching of anthropology.

Archaeology

Archaeology is sometimes grouped with physical anthropology for teaching purposes. It is clearly cultural rather than biological, however, for the archaeologist studies the information about human cultures that can be gained from the careful digging up of ancient dwellings, monuments, objects of art, tools, weapons, and other works of man covered over by the soils of time.

Typical course offerings in archaeology can include: "New World Archaeology" (concerned with the prehistoric remains of American Indian cultures); "Old World Prehistory" (study of the stone tools, cave art, and other evidence about human life during the million or more years of the great Ice Ages); "Beginnings of Near Eastern Civilization"; and various specializations within these broad studies.

Since archaeologists are concerned with "digging up man's past," they have important connections with history and historians. As a matter of fact, the "classical archaeologists," who dig in the ruins of ancient civilizations of the Mediterranean and Middle East (Troy, Crete, the tombs of Egypt, etc.), are usually found in departments of history or the classics, rather than in anthropology. Concern with the evidence of the past found in the earth's crust also links archaeologists with geologists, palaeontologists, palaeobotanists, and the geophysicists.

Linguistics

"Linguistics" is the study of language—man's highly elaborated system of communication. This study is not concerned with learning to speak foreign languages fluently but rather is aimed at accurate scientific description and comparison of languages. Probably the earliest strong interest in linguistics was developed around the study of the relationships among languages, particularly when it was discovered that most of the languages of Europe, though mutually unintelligible, are descended from a single common ancestor language—ancient Indo-European.

Recent developments in linguistics have brought the linguists into increasing contact with psychologists, philosophers, and mathematicians, as they pursue such topics as psycholinguistics, metalinguistics, semantics, and communications theory.

Ethnology

"Peoples and Cultures of Africa," "Ethnology of Oceania," "North American Indians" and a number of similar course titles illustrate the cultural anthropologist's concern with the infinite varieties of human behavior that have been found on the face of our globe. From this world-wide range of cultures and peoples, anthropologists search for similarities and differences that provide clues to understanding "human nature" and human culture history.

The courses in which cultural anthropologists present their systematic comparisons and theoretical researches are variously entitled "Comparative Economics," "Comparative Religion," "Culture Change," "Primitive Law and Government," "Social Structure," and so on. When psychological theory is systematically interwoven with these comparative ethnological data, we find courses entitled "Culture and Personality" and "Psychological Anthropology."

Whenever an anthropologist is engaged in straightforward description of the cultural patterns of a given society he is concerned with "ethnography." When his materials are organized in terms of social systems, we can label the research (or the course) "Social Anthropology," indicating (among other things) the influence on Americans of some very interesting developments in British anthropology of the past forty years. Other diverse interests of anthropologists are made clear by the names of their course listings: for example, "Ethnomusicology," "Comparative Folklore," and "Primitive Art." Courses in which anthropological knowledge and theory are centered on the practical problems of our complex age are usually titled "Applied Anthropology."

ANTHROPOLOGY IS FUNDAMENTALLY CROSS-CULTURAL

Very often the first sign of an anthropologist-to-be is a young boy's or girl's fascination with Indians, lost continents, explorations in Africa, and exotic island peoples of the South Seas. The same kind of fascination with the "unusual" and "different" among peoples and cultures has spurred many anthropologists to their first extensive field work. When a thirst for systematic observation and comparative research are grafted onto the earlier romantic impulses, the motivations for a mature anthropology begin to emerge.

Curiosity and fascination with the exotic are not the main justifications for the anthropologist's interests in primitive peoples,[2] however. The more fundamental explanation is that non-Western societies provide a great range of behavioral diversity. Economic institutions, family organization, religious beliefs and practices, magic, artistic achievements, and personality types of every description provide the evidence for establishing the constants and the variants of human culture. The anthropologist feels that the fundamental principles of cultural and social systems can be discovered only through study of the whole range of human behavior patterns. Still another reason for the anthropologist's study of non-Western societies is that these provide him with a sort of "laboratory" setting, where something approaching the total scope of a cultural system can be observed in a relatively compact, localized community that is not just a fragment of a huge, modern society.

Some anthropologists have maintained that their field of study is concerned exclusively with primitive peoples, but most anthropologists see their discipline as a general study of bio-cultural man; and recent anthropological research has diverged sharply from the earlier concentration on pre-literate societies. A very large part of the anthropological research of the postwar period has been in the subcommunities and specialized segments of large, literate

---

2 The word "primitive" in casual conversation seems to refer most usually to peoples and practices that "civilized" Europeans and Americans regard as strange, quaint, and (generally) inferior. The anthropologist, when he uses the expression at all, defines "primitive peoples" as people who have no written language—hence, "pre-literate" people. Anthropological researchers generally avoid making value judgments about supposedly "inferior" or "irrational" or "backward" behavior.

societies. These include work on rural communities of modern Europe, Latin America, Japan, and India, in addition to anthropological study of topics like "the culture of a psychiatric hospital," "city taverns," "themes in French culture," and "the American kinship system."

THE INTEGRATION OF ANTHROPOLOGY

It is evident that anthropology—however specific it may often be in dealing with data—aims at being ultimately a co-ordinating science, somewhat as a legitimate holding corporation co-ordinates constituent companies. We anthropologists will never know China as intensively as a Sinologist does, or prices, credit, and banking as well as an economist, or heredity with the fulness of the genetic biologist. But we face what these more intensive scholars only glance at intermittently and tangentially, if at all: to try to understand in some measure how Chinese civilization and economics and human heredity, and some dozens of other highly developed special bodies of knowledge, do indeed interrelate in being all parts of "man"— flowing out of man, centered in him, products of him.[3]

With these words the late Alfred L. Kroeber, one of the foremost anthropologists of this century, expressed the idea that the stuff of anthropology is drawn from many different areas of knowledge. The research interests and types of courses taught by anthropologists reflect this great diversity, but in many situations today there are tendencies toward the fragmentation of the discipline. Physical anthropology, for example, is becoming increasingly specialized and complex in its researches on the physiology, anatomy, and genetic attributes of man. Most cultural anthropologists find themselves farther and farther out of touch with the newest research and information in this field. At the same time, scholars in physical anthropology experience great pressures to concentrate their energies on the rapidly developing areas of radiobiology, the chemistry and physics of human genetics, and related fields. Thus they may become comparative strangers to the interests and researches of the linguists, cultural anthropologists, and archaeologists who are their fellow staff members in departments of anthropology.

Also, the study of linguistics has become highly specialized, with an intricate vocabulary of description, semimathematical

[3] A. L. Kroeber (ed.), *Anthropology Today* (Chicago: University of Chicago Press, 1953), p. xiv. Copyright 1953. All rights reserved.

modes of analysis of language structure, and extremely complex philosophical and psychological arguments over fundamental assumptions in the field.

As we view the natural history of different branches of science and philosophy, we see that diversification and separation of fields of study is a natural result of increased knowledge about the world in which we live. It is easy, therefore, to argue that gradual splitting up of the different branches of anthropology into separate disciplines would be just as natural as the differentiation of chemistry, physics, and biology from the earlier unity of general science. But most anthropologists, especially in the United States, cling stubbornly to the "holistic principle" as stated by Dr. Kroeber. For, despite all tendencies toward specialization, the strong interrelatedness of man's physical characteristics and his behavioral systems cannot be ignored. From whatever angle the nature of the human animal is approached, there is no denying that man's economic behavior, religious institutions, and other aspects of culture are deeply influenced by his psychobiological characteristics. Similarly, man's body as a physical system is affected by his religion, his occupation, his family, and other social and cultural facts.

One area of study that graphically illustrates the integration of the study of man is concerned with the problems of mental illness. In postwar years important advances have been made in the development of a holistic theory of psychiatric disorder. The development of drugs and other organic treatments demonstrates the relationship of man's biological attributes to his psychological functioning. Theoretical developments in the area of psychosomatic medicine offer additional evidence of these linkages. At the same time, studies of mental disorders among the Eskimos, peoples in Africa, Asia, and other areas, and evidence of different rates and kinds of mental illness in subsections of our own society show the importance of social and cultural factors in problems of mental health.

The integration of biological and cultural data in research on mental illness is particularly well illustrated in Anthony F. C. Wallace's analysis of a mental disorder called *pibloktoq*, found among the Greenland Eskimos. *Pibloktoq* is characterized by compulsive mimicking behavior, "speaking in tongues," shouting, weeping, tearing off clothing, and running away naked in the arctic cold. Rejecting a wholly psychoanalytic interpretation for this disorder, Wallace suggests that it is related to periodic calcium deficiencies in the Eskimo diet. Particular social circumstances trigger the breakdown, however, and the specific contents of the aberrant behavior must be understood in terms of Eskimo psychological and cultural patterns. Clearly, research on problems of this sort requires close collaboration among biological, psychological, and cultural sciences.

RELATIONSHIPS WITH OTHER SOCIAL SCIENCES

In practice there is a good deal of both theoretical and practical overlap between anthropology and sociology. And the areas of common interest seem to have increased considerably in the past fifteen or twenty years. Nonetheless, some general differences separate the interests of *most* anthropologists from those of *most* sociologists. These differences in tendency include:

1. Most anthropologists prefer to study non-Western peoples (though there are many exceptions); most sociologists prefer to study aspects of Western society and culture. (But growing numbers of sociologists are now immersed in studies of African, Indian, Chinese, and other societies, and more anthropologists are looking at their own cultures.)
2. Most anthropologists prefer to do research on small communities, by means of observations and interviews of people in face-to-face contact. Most sociologists prefer to study larger segments of social systems, using information gathered on questionnaires or extracted from statistics on population, crime rates, employment figures, voting records, and so on. In general, sociologists feel much more at home using statistical analysis than do anthropologists.
3. Anthropologists include physical anthropology as an important part of their science; sociologists concentrate their studies nearly exclusively on social aspects of man.
4. Most anthropologists consider human culture history to be a central concern of the discipline; the majority of sociologists leave historical studies to others, preferring modern social institutions for research topics.

The differences between anthropology and psychology are much more clearly observable, though again there are growing areas of overlap. Psychologists usually study the behavior of individuals in carefully defined laboratory or experimental situations; thus, psychology is much more an experimental science than is anthropology. Psychologists are, in the main, even less interested than sociologists in study of non-Western peoples. However, the rapidly developing field of social psychology includes cross-cultural studies and other features that are very close to the interests of psychologically-oriented anthropologists. Anthropologists and psychologists also have common interests and much potential for joint research on the physiology of the human brain and nervous system. A somewhat unexpected area of co-operation has developed between psychology and anthropology in laboratory and field studies of monkeys and apes.

Anthropology also shares notable similarities of interest with geography. Studies of the spread of domestication of plants and animals; adaptation of peoples to particular kinds of physical environments; social and cultural characteristics of pastoral (animal herding) societies, and a great many other areas of research are studied simultaneously by geographers and anthropologists. In topics such as Islamic culture history, Chinese culture and society, and Latin American culture history we often find anthropologists and historians working on very similar research interests, though methods of study may be different. The full range of anthropological interests and research links the work of anthropologists with that of scholars in many other fields. This is natural and expected, for all scholars accept the principle of the interconnection of the universe, the unity of all life on earth, and the oneness of human history and society. Special areas of study labeled with the names of various "ologies" are, after all, artificial segments of information chopped out of the unified web of events and things. If scholars paid careful heed to the artificial boundaries between areas of study, we might still be in the Dark Ages of human knowledge.

SUMMARY

Since anthropology is "the study of man," including human social, cultural, psychological, and physical characteristics, anthropological study is partly biological science, partly social science, and in part included among the humanities. In the main lines of their studies, anthropologists may be distinguishable from sociologists, psychologists, physiologists, zoologists, geographers, historians, and others; but the wide-ranging interests of individual scholars make any clear boundaries among these several disciplines impossible to draw. Some of the most exciting areas of modern research are those that play havoc with the boundaries among the various disciplines. Studies of mental health and mental disorder, for example, involve the work of physiologists, psychiatrists, psychologists, sociologists, anthropologists, geneticists, biochemists, and social workers. The general areas of human evolution and cultural history similarly combine work from dozens of different branches of science and humanities.

In the welter of interlaced scientific and historical studies anthropologists have attempted to maintain a broad, holistic approach to their work. Narrow specializations have generally been avoided, and the splitting of anthropology into separated subcompartments has also been avoided, although the strains involved in this unity of anthropology sometimes show on the faces of weary and harassed students who must spread their studies over such wide ranges of knowledge.

Suggested Reading

Hoebel, E. Adamson. *Man in the Primitive World* (2nd ed.). New York: McGraw-Hill Book Co., Inc., 1958.

Written as an elementary college textbook, this work is extremely well illustrated and exciting reading. The major sub-areas of anthropology are discussed, and important concepts and information in each area are presented simply and clearly.

*Kluckhohn, Clyde. *Mirror For Man*. New York: Fawcett Publications, Inc., 1960.

This is a well-rounded, readable introduction to anthropology written by one of the most prominent anthropologists of recent decades.

*Oliver, Douglas. *Invitation to Anthropology*. ("American Museum Science Books.") Garden City: The Natural History Press, 1964.

Dr. Oliver explains very briefly and succinctly the fundamental ideas, methods, and schools of thought in modern anthropology.

---

* Paperback.

Advanced Reading

*Kroeber, A. L. *Anthropology, Biology and Race,* Vol. I. *Anthropology, Culture Patterns and Processes,* Vol. II. New York: Harbinger Paperbacks, 1963.

This classic compendium by "the grand old man" of anthropology was first published in 1948, but is far from out of date.

*Tax, Sol (ed.). *Anthropology Today—Selections.* Chicago: University of Chicago Press, 1962.

These "inventory papers" on various aspects of anthropological method and theory were put together for a high-level conference in 1953. Although much has happened in anthropology since that time, the collection gives an impressive survey of the state of anthropology in the postwar period.

chapter two

The
History of
Anthropology

ANTHROPOLOGY AMONG THE ANCIENTS

They have, however, one singular custom in which they differ
from every other nation in the world. They take the mother's
and not the father's name. Ask a Lycian who he is, and he answers
by giving his own name, that of his mother, and so on in the female
line. Moreover, if a free woman marry a man who is a slave, their
children are full citizens; but if a free man marry a foreign woman
or live with a concubine, even though he be the first person in the
state, the children forfeit all the rights of citizenship.[1]

This concise description of a matrilineal, or "mother-right,"
social system is from the ethnological observations of Herodotus,
the Greek historian, philosopher, and anthropologist (484–424 B.C.).
Herodotus traveled widely in the then known world, and he
observed firsthand many different peoples and customs. Like modern
anthropologists, he interviewed "key informants" and recorded
their statements for posterity.
Concerning ethnocentrism, Herodotus wrote:

. . . if one were to offer men to choose out of all the customs in the
world such as seemed to them best, they would examine the whole
number, and end by preferring their own; so convinced are they
that their own usages far surpass those of all others . . .[2]

---

[1] E. H. Blakeney (ed.), *The History of Herodotus*, 2 vols., trans. George
Rawlinson (London: Everyman's Library, 1910), I, 89.
[2] *Ibid.*, pp. 229–30.

Although Herodotus and a few other ancient Greeks were the first men to embark on a naturalistic study of man, we must turn to the Roman, Tacitus, for our best example of an early "ethnographic monograph" about a particular "primitive" culture. In his *Germania* (98 A.D.) Tacitus described the character, manners, and geographical setting of the German tribes. He wrote to warn fellow Romans of the strength and spirit of the Germans, for he saw them as uncorrupted barbarians who would bring about the downfall of a rapidly degenerating Rome. He noted with admiration that "no one in Germany finds vice amusing, or calls it 'up-to-date' to debauch and be debauched." [3] Also:

> For all that, marriage in Germany is austere, and there is no feature in their morality that deserves higher praise. They are almost unique among barbarians in being satisfied with one wife each. The exceptions, which are exceedingly rare, are of men who receive offers of many wives because of their rank. There is no question of sexual passion. The dowry is brought by husband to wife, not by wife to husband.[4]

After Tacitus, up to the thirteenth and fourteenth centuries, there appeared few men who attempted dispassionate observation and explanation of human behavior and society. The development of a strong religious movement, dating from St. Augustine, drew men toward more theological and metaphysical interpretations of human behavior. Any naturalistic, empirical investigation of man's nature and surroundings came to be discouraged by threats of harassment and persecution.

THE GREAT TRAVELERS: MARCO POLO, IBN BATUTA, IBN KHALDUN

In the thirteenth and fourteenth centuries there were a few isolated instances of "proto-anthropological" writing. The famous Marco Polo, having traveled in China and much of the rest of Asia for more than twenty years (1271-1295), transmitted to posterity a wealth of knowledge of peoples and customs far beyond the imaginations of his Italian contemporaries. Here is a fragment from his observations about the Tartars of Central Asia:

---

[3] *Tacitus on Britain and Germany*, trans. H. Mattingly (London: Penguin Classics, 1948), p. 117.
[4] *Ibid.*, p. 115.

They have circular houses made of wood and covered with felt, which they carry with them on four-wheeled wagons wherever they go. For the framework of rods is so neatly and skillfully constructed that it is light to carry . . . and I assure you that the womenfolk buy and sell and do all that is needful for their husbands and households. For the men do not bother themselves with anything but hunting and warfare and falconry . . . They have no objection to eating the flesh of horses and dogs and drinking mare's milk . . . Not for anything in the world would one of them touch another's wife; they are too well assured that such a deed is wrongful and disgraceful . . .[5]

Ibn Batuta (1304-1378), the greatest Arab traveler of the Middle Ages, set off from his native North Africa on a series of travels to Russia, China, India, Sumatra, Cambodia, and then into sub-Saharan West Africa, including Timbuktu. The main lines of his twenty-eight years of travel covered something like 75,000 miles. Then by royal order he dictated his narrative to Mohammed Ibn Juzai. Ibn Batuta's narrative reveals much information about relationships among the various Islamic governments of his time, as well as details of Islamic religious and cultural practices.

About the same time, another Arab scholar, Ibn Khaldun, was collecting observations and writing about the nature of human society. He was not just a collector of information and observations, like Polo and Ibn Batuta, but must be considered a profound social scientist. From his own rich experiences in various Islamic governments, plus his extensive reading and observations, he attempted to organize "a study of human society in all its different forms, the nature and characteristics of each of these forms, and the laws governing its development."[6] Some of Ibn Khaldun's principles are remarkably modern, though written over 500 years ago:

1. Social phenomena obey laws, which are sufficiently constant to cause social events to follow regular, well-defined patterns and sequences.

2. These laws operate on masses, and cannot be significantly influenced by isolated individuals. (He gives the example of the reformer's attempts to rejuvenate a corrupt state. These reform efforts meet with little success; the individual's efforts are submerged by overwhelming social forces.)

---

[5] *The Travels of Marco Polo*, trans. R. E. Latham (London: Penguin Classics, 1958), p. 67.
[6] *An Arab Philosophy of History*, trans. and arr. by Charles Issawi (London: John Murray, 1950), pp. 7–9.

3. Social laws can be discovered only by gathering large numbers of facts, from which sequences and correlations can be observed.
4. Similar social laws operate in societies of the same kind of structures, however separated in time and space. (He notes similarities among nomadic Bedouins, Kurds, and Berbers.)
5. Societies are not static, for social forms change and evolve.
6. These are all *social* laws, not merely reflections of biological or physical factors.

THE AGE OF DISCOVERY

In the fifteenth century, a series of important developments opened the way for large additions to man's knowledge of man. A successful printing press was developed (1446); knowledge of paper was brought to Western Europe by the Arabs; and the fall of Constantinople (1453) brought a migration of Aristotelian scholars into Western Europe. All these developments had a catalytic effect on scholarship in the West.

Also, by the end of the fifteenth century, Portuguese, Spanish, and other seagoers had ventured far into hitherto unknown oceans, reaching the New World. There began a rapid accumulation of new knowledge about the peoples of the world—the Red Indians of America, island peoples of the South Seas, seal-and-caribou-hunting peoples of Greenland, the richly varied populations of India and southeast Asia, and the large populations of Negroes south of the Sahara desert barrier.

Theologically derived doctrines had divided all of mankind into descendants of Shem, Ham, and Japhet, all descended from Adam. The newly discovered varieties of peoples seemed not to fit very well into these categories. The first Spaniards active in exploring (and plundering) the New World claimed that the American Indians were not descendants of Adam, hence were outside the grace of God; this supposedly justified the cruelties carried out by the conquistadors. In 1512 the Pope declared that the American Indians were, indeed, descendants of Adam, hence entitled to be treated according to the same moral principles as Europeans. Explorers and exploiters continued to treat the "natives" as fair game, but individual Catholic missionaries often worked hard to protect the human rights of the Indians. Meanwhile, many scholars in Europe, including Paracelsus and Giordano Bruno, continued to maintain that

Ethiopians, South Sea Islanders, and other such physically "different" peoples were not the same species as Europeans.

Richard Hakluyt's *Divers Voyages Touching the Discovery of America* (1582) is perhaps the most famous of the many collections of geographical and anthropological information that began to be available to scholars of the sixteenth, seventeenth and eighteenth centuries. Other well-known works include the *Historia de Gentibus Septentrionalis* ("History of the People of the North") by Claus Magnus (1555), the mammoth seventy-three volume collection of *Jesuit Relations* gathered by missionaries in the New World between 1610 and 1791, Captain Cook's *Voyages* (1770's and 1780's), P. S. Pallas' account of his Russian journey (1771-76), and D. Crantz's *History of Greenland* (1767).

Ethnographic data from these volumes began to appear in the arguments of the Enlightenment philosophers. John Locke quoted from the *Jesuit Relations* in discussing his "social contract," and J. J. Rousseau introduced the idea of the "noble savage" into philosophical speculation, using the Carib Indians of Venezuela for his model.

THE RISE OF ANTHROPOLOGY

Those same philosophers of the Enlightenment had developed the ideas of progress and evolution that came to be the central focus of nineteenth-century anthropological theory, and many bits and pieces of anthropological ideas date back to those earlier centuries. But the story of human biological and cultural development began to take on a recognizable pattern only in the nineteenth century. Before that time, not only was descriptive information lacking, but obstacles of theological dogma had to be overcome as well.

Up to the beginning of the nineteenth century, many or most scholars dealing with human cultural diversity and history had accepted the age of the earth as pronounced by Archbishop Ussher in 1650. The good Archbishop had calculated from a careful study of the scriptures that the world had been created by God just 4,004 years before the birth of Christ, to which the theologian Dr. Lightfoot had added the demonstration that "heaven and earth, center and circumference, were created together, in the same instant, and clouds full of water . . . [and that] this work took place and man was created by the Trinity on the twenty-third of October, 4004 B.C. at nine o'clock in the morning." [7]

In the 1830's and 1840's, however, the French Abbe Boucher de Perthes discovered numbers of stone tools in the gravels of the river Somme, near Paris, and he began to insist on the immense antiquity of these works of man. Great theological and scientific argument raged, especially in France and England, over the age of these archaeological materials. Other significant archaeological finds were made both in France and England, and as early as 1825 a rhinoceros tooth had been found with a flint weapon in Kent's Cavern in England, by the Rev. J. MacEnery. The rapid accumulation of evidence about the Stone Age of man seriously undermined the orthodox, Biblical chronology of human cultural history.

Another striking development in the accumulating evidence concerning man's antiquity took place in a little river valley near Dusseldorf, in Germany. There, in 1857, were found portions of a human skeleton with features very different from those of modern man. The skull was massive, somewhat flattened on top, with extremely heavy brow ridges. The German doctor who first wrote about these human fossil remains described them as belonging to a "barbarous and savage race . . . the most ancient memorial of the early inhabitants of Europe." [8] This immensely important fossil had been found in the valley of the Neander River, hence its name—Neandertal Man.

By 1859, the year of publication of Darwin's *The Origin of Species*, leading scientists of Western Europe were ready to accept the theory that earth and man are very old; that the relative age of rocks, soil, and human artifacts can be read from their positions in the layers, or strata, laid down on the surface of the earth following known geological principles; and that the stone tools and skeletal remains from various sites in England, France, and elsewhere are evidence of the beginnings of human biological and cultural history dating from hundreds of thousands of years ago. Darwin's famous theory of natural selection provided a way of explaining man's relation to his natural world, and for understanding the relationship of Neandertal Man (and other such fossils) to modern *Homo sapiens*. Some scientists were quick to apply the basic principles of evolution to the nonbiological cultural materials as well.

---

[7] From *Man and His Gods,* p. 324, by Homer W. Smith. Copyright 1953 by Homer W. Smith. Reprinted by permission of Little, Brown and Company.
[8] T. K. Penniman, *A Hundred Years of Anthropology* (2nd ed., revised; London: Gerald Duckworth and Co., Ltd., 1952), p. 68.

EARLY APPLIED ANTHROPOLOGY

In Tasmania, where thousands were hunted down like beasts and shot, by 1835 only 203 aboriginals were left, the pitiful remnant of thousands. The last pure-blooded Tasmanian died in 1861. On the continent they did not fare much better. [Australian] Sheepherders, in order to clear the grazing-grounds more rapidly, offered them, in apparent friendliness, cakes of flour dosed with arsenic, and thus poisoned off black humanity like ground squirrels. Other ingenious native-exterminators poisoned the waterholes.[9]

The slaughter of aborigines, along with the vast inhumanity of the slave trade, aroused the consciences of many humanitarians in England and on the Continent. In 1837 the Aborigines Protection Society was founded in London, and a year later, with similar humane intentions, the Ethnological Society in Paris. The *Journal of the Ethnological Society* of London, in 1856, carried this statement:

Ethnology is now generally recognized as having the strongest claims in our attention, not merely as it tends to gratify the curiosity of those who love to look into Nature's works, but also as being of great practical importance, especially in this country, whose numerous colonies and extensive commerce bring it into contact with so many varieties of the human species differing in their physical and moral qualities both from each other and from ourselves.[10]

The study of anthropology developed, therefore, from a fusion of theoretical and practical interests. On the one hand was the scholarly curiosity concerning the Stone Age, the rise of ancient civilizations, and the "strange and exotic" customs of diverse living peoples. At the same time, many of the early anthropologists were imbued with the conviction that knowledge of human cultures would bring immediate practical advantages to men—in the reduction of human cruelty, misery, and ignorance.

THE DOCTRINE OF CULTURAL EVOLUTION

Although anthropological theories of the evolution of culture were given a strong boost by the publication of Darwin's *The Origin of Species*, we should understand that the concepts of cul-

---

[9] H. R. Hays, *From Ape to Angel* (New York: Alfred A. Knopf, Inc., 1958), p. 85.
[10] Pp. 294–97.

tural evolution that dominated anthropological thinking in the nineteenth century were not directly an outgrowth of Darwinian ideas. The philosophers of the Enlightenment—especially Turgot and Condorcet—are principal sources for many of the ideas that composed the theory of cultural evolution. They held that the history of humans can be described as progress (betterment) from simple beginnings to our complex civilization. They set forth supposed stages through which human culture had progressed, starting with the creation, the fall, and the flood, followed by man's organization into small groups of hunters and gatherers, then the development of pastoralism, the inventions of agriculture and the idea of private property, the growth of villages, division of labor, and thence to modern civilization.

Lewis Henry Morgan

L. H. Morgan (1818-1881) is considered to be the founding father of American anthropology. Morgan was born in upstate New York, where he studied law at Union College in Schenectady, and then settled down to law practice, business, politics, and anthropological study in Rochester. As a young man, Morgan had founded the Order of the Gordian Knot at Aurora, organized around ideas of Greek mythology, secret rites, sacred paraphernalia, and other similar trappings. Somewhat later, the society was reorganized around American Indian ritual and mythology, as the Grand Order of the Iroquois. In collecting information about the Iroquois for these social activities, Morgan became interested in the Iroquois themselves and began to gather materials for more serious purposes. Soon he was deeply involved in trying to help the Iroquois against unscrupulous land-grabbers, meanwhile continuing his ethnographic notes. His *League of the Iroquois* (1851), the first fairly comprehensive monograph on a North American Indian tribe, resulted from these efforts.

In working with the Iroquois, Morgan had discovered some rather "peculiar" things about the kinship terms these people used in referring to their various relatives. An Iroquois individual called his mother's sister by the same word as he used in referring to his mother. Also, the father's brother—indeed quite a number of other male paternal relatives—were called by the same word as that used for one's father. Furthermore, the whole of Iroquois society was organized into matrilineal clans (kinship groups claiming descent through females only); and when a couple married they generally

TABLE 1

Morgan's Stages of Evolution

(Read from bottom up)

Stages	Cultural Example	Differentiating Characteristics
Civilization	Europeans, Americans	begins after the alphabet was invented
Higher Barbarism	Greeks of ancient time	begins with use of iron
Middle Barbarism	Zuni, Hopi Indians	begins with domestication of animals and plants
Lower Barbarism	Iroquois Indians	begins with invention of pottery
Higher Savagery	Polynesians	begins with use of bow and arrow
Middle Savagery	Australian aborigines	begins with fish diet, use of fire and speech
Lower Savagery	no known examples	before fire and speech were invented

settled down with the bride's kin rather than joining the man's kin group or establishing a household of their own.

Morgan searched for an explanation of the Iroquois patterns of kinship terminology, and thought he found it in the idea of "survivals." That is, if all human societies (including the Iroquois) had passed through an evolutionary stage of "group marriage"— the union of several men with several women, the Iroquois called several people "mother" and numbers of older males "father" as a relic from that bygone stage of society.

Morgan collected information on kinship systems from many parts of the world and wove them into the fabric of Enlightenment theorizing about human progress, adding many innovations of his own. Table 1 shows the main stages of human cultural evolution from Morgan's most famous book, *Ancient Society*.[11]

The basic philosophical premises of Morgan's evolutionary system are similar to the ideas underlying the writings of most other well-known anthropologists of the nineteenth century. They assumed

---

[11] New York: Holt, Rinehart & Winston, Inc., 1877.

that all men are rational beings who strive to improve themselves. They assumed that mankind is part of nature, hence developing in accordance with natural laws. These laws of the universe were considered to be unchanging through time. In general, they felt that evolution proceeds from simple to complex, from unorganized to organized, and, especially, that this development is directly associated with betterment—that evolution is simultaneously progress, the march toward human perfection.

In 1879, Morgan was elected president of the American Association for the Advancement of Science, and in the same year he was offered the directorship of the newly created Bureau of American Ethnology. Morgan was ill, however, and urged his friend, Colonel John Wesley Powell, to take that important position. Morgan was the acknowledged leader of American anthropology when he died in 1881.

Edward B. Tylor

Edward B. Tylor was Morgan's English counterpart. In his most important book, *Primitive Culture* (1871), he elaborated his version of the story of evolution with special concentration on religion. He believed that the earliest primitive religion had been "animism"—the belief that persons, animals, and even trees and stones have indwelling spirits or souls. The origin of this belief and hence the origin of religion, Tylor theorized, is to be found in man's seeking rationally to explain what happens in dreaming and death.

During the nineteenth century, theologians argued, following Biblical interpretation, that man had fallen from grace and that primitive peoples had degenerated the furthest from the original high culture of paradise. Tylor and the evolutionists claimed, on the other hand, that primitive peoples like the Australians are examples of the rude beginnings of all mankind and that everywhere there is progress from savagery toward civilization, though some peoples (possibly due to isolation and other factors) have not progressed as far as others in this evolution.

Although he held no university degree, Tylor became the foremost anthropologist in England and was appointed the first Professor of Anthropology at Oxford (1896). He quite accurately predicted that the new science would develop "from a derided byway of truth to a time when its help and decisions are sought for by governments."

Other nineteenth-century scholars contributed important ideas to the growing science. In England, Sir John Lubbock coined the now familiar terms *palaeolithic* and *neolithic* in the course of his studies of prehistory; Sir Henry Maine, in his *Ancient Law* (1861), laid the foundations for the comparative study of legal systems; later, Sir James G. Frazer collected and organized an amazing mass of information on magic and religion, widely known in the several editions of his *Golden Bough*. A Swiss jurist, J. J. Bachofen, published a richly documented argument for an early stage of matrilineality in human culture history (*Das Mutterrecht*, 1861). And in Germany, the tireless traveler and writer, Adolph Bastian, is honored as the founder of the Royal Ethnological Museum in Berlin and co-founder of the Berlin Society for Anthropology, Ethnology, and Prehistory.

REACTION TO EVOLUTION

As the nineteenth century neared its close, some anthropologists began to have serious doubts about Morgan's and Tylor's theories of cultural evolution. These anti-evolutionist scholars doubted that all human societies pass through the same stages. They denied that human history always has represented progress, and they advanced the idea that human culture history is best understood as the result of complex diffusion of cultural elements among human groups.

The most extreme anti-evolutionists were the Englishmen, W. J. Perry and Sir Grafton Elliot Smith, who claimed that peoples of the world are so unimaginative that practically all cultural development must have been invented in one place—Egypt—and diffused from there throughout the world. The metallurgy, agriculture, architecture, complex society, religious practices, and other cultural attainments of Maya, Aztec, and Inca civilizations, for example, they explained as inventions borrowed from the center of all things —Egypt.

Austrian anthropologists also developed an anti-evolutionist school of thought in the beginning of the twentieth century, somewhat less extreme than the Egypt-centered theories. Fritz Graebner and Peter Wilhelm Schmidt, leaders of the "Vienna school," believed that original human culture developed somewhere in Asia, and from this *Urkultur* there developed several distinct *Kulturkriese* ("culture complexes") in different environments. Great migrations of peoples carried these ancient *Kulturkreise* into widely separated parts of the globe. For example, the *exogamous matrilineal kulturkreise*, which has hoe-agriculture, plank boats, moon mythology, rectangular houses with gabled roofs, and men's secret societies, was supposedly carried to both the New Guinea area and to Africa. The *Kulturkreise* anthropologists have been heavily criticized for weaknesses of theory, but they frequently are applauded for their extensive field work.

In American anthropology, one single individual stands out as the man who "overthrew" cultural evolutionist theories. The man was Franz Boas. Boas was educated in Germany, taking his degree in geography and physics. His professors had guided him to a firm empiricism, insisting that facts come first and theory later. During geographical field work in Baffinland (1883-84), he realized that his main interests tended toward the study of people instead of climate and physical landscape, so he became an anthropologist, ultimately taking a joint position at Columbia University and the American Museum of Natural History (1895). Columbia University quickly became a focal point of anthropological activity, as growing numbers of Boasian students began extensive field studies among American Indians. Clark Wissler, A. L. Kroeber, Robert Lowie, Margaret Mead, Ruth Benedict, and Melville Herskovits are among the better known of Boas' students.

It is hard for us to realize that in the 1890's—a relatively few years ago—there were still free bands of Indians, threatened but not yet crushed by the waves of covered wagoners, gold miners, railroad workers, army troops and other settlers of the American West. To Boas and his students, every day spent in one's library theorizing about evolution, culture history, and other vague, abstract ideas, meant one day's loss of priceless, irretrievable ethnographic data. So they went out in the summers and at every other conceivable opportunity, with small amounts of expense money provided by the Museum, to collect information and cultural artifacts from the Dakota, Cheyenne, Blackfoot, Crow, Apache, and other groups that only a few years previously had hunted buffalo, raided each other's horse herds, and fought American army units (and one another) in the Great Plains. Boas himself carried out extensive field work among the Kwakiutl and other tribes of the British Columbia seacoast.

From the accumulating masses of ethnographic data on American Indians, Boas and his followers shaped a strongly anti-evolutionary theory. They denounced Morgan's stages as figments of imagination, unsupported by evidence. The complexities of ethnographic information do not fit into neat stages, they claimed. For example, several Indian tribes of the Great Plains had given up settled agricultural life in favor of nomadic buffalo-hunting—

strictly the reverse of the Morgan-Tylor evolutionary sequences. They saw the history of man as a sort of "tree of culture," with fantastically complex branching, intertwining, and budding off— each branch representing a uniquely different cultural complex, to be understood in terms of its own unique history rather than compared to cultural complexes in other world regions in some grand scheme of "stages of evolution." Some of the differences between this new "culture historical" and the evolutionary perspective on human culture can be seen in Figure 1.

Other points at which this new "American school" of anthropology differed with the evolutionists include:

Denial of the idea that development could be equated with progress or betterment.

Refusal to consider widely separated cultures as representatives of broad "culture types," such as the all-embracing category, "savagery."

Organization of the world of ethnographic data into "culture areas," each thought to be unique in culture history, with a resulting distinctive array of culture elements, or traits.

The differences between evolutionist and anti-evolutionist views have often obscured certain fundamental agreements. Both emphasized the rationality and humanity of primitive peoples; they were in thorough agreement that cultural differences are due to culture history and not biological inequalities; and both schools of thought were fundamentally opposed to the theological view that primitive peoples have "degenerated" from a state of original paradise. Evolutionists and anti-evolutionists alike constructed their theories by interrelating evidence from human biology, archaeology, study of languages, and ethnography.

PSYCHOLOGICAL AND CONFIGURATIONAL STUDIES

It is always the individual that really thinks and acts and dreams and revolts.[12]

This credo was written by Edward Sapir, one of Boas' most brilliant students, in reaction to what he felt to be the depersonalization inherent in the study of culture complexes, diffusion of

---

[12] Edward Sapir, "Do We Need a Superorganic?" *American Anthropologist,* XIX (1917), 441–47.

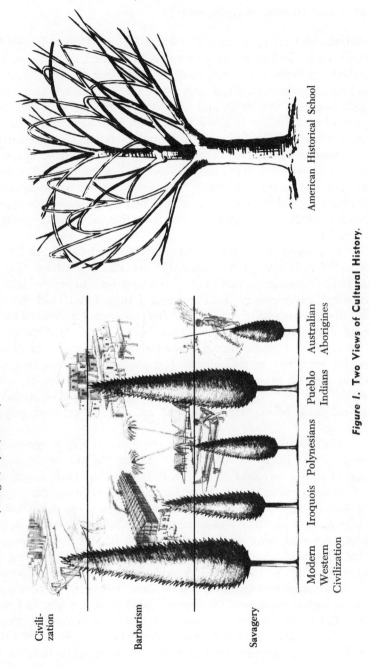

The Tree of Culture

American Historical School

Unilinear Evolution
(Morgan, Tylor, *et al.*)

Civili-
zation

Barbarism

Savagery

Modern   Iroquois   Polynesians   Pueblo   Australian
Western   Indians   Aborigines
Civilization

Figure 1. **Two Views of Cultural History.**

customs, and reconstruction of culture history. Human beings had come to be looked on as passive "culture carriers" without individual significance for the study of anthropology. In a series of papers and seminars, Sapir and a few other American anthropologists began in the 1920's and 30's to work toward an inclusion of psychological study in anthropology. One of Sapir's articles was aptly entitled, "Why Cultural Anthropology Needs the Psychiatrist."

Another of Boas' students, Margaret Mead, became interested in psychiatry and the relationships of personality and culture; for her first major field work, she set out to study psychological problems of adolescents among the Samoans. *Coming of Age in Samoa* (1928) is a pioneer effort in this new anthropological direction.

In a series of seminars during the 1930's at Columbia University, Ralph Linton (anthropologist) and Abram Kardiner (psychiatrist) collaborated in producing a new approach to psychologically-oriented anthropology. Kardiner and Linton formulated the idea of "basic personality" as a unifying concept for understanding man and culture. The "basic personality" of a given people is that pattern of psychological characteristics common to all or most of the members of the society brought about by similarities in child training practices. The basic personality of a society, once established, is reflected in many areas of custom—particularly in religious beliefs and practices, art, mythology, and popular fantasies.

Cora DuBois applied this general frame of theory in her colorful study of *The People of Alor* (1944). Among the Alorese, located on one of the easternmost islands of Indonesia, Dr. DuBois gathered information about child training and individual dreams, biographies of individuals, as well as data about economic, social, and ritual-cultural patterns. She also obtained responses to Rorschach (ink-blot) tests and other psychological materials. Her findings suggest that Alorese children suffer great anxieties about their feeding and care, leading to food-anxieties and other important personality characteristics among the adults. These elements of personality are in turn explanations for themes about food, hunger, and other anxieties in their religious rituals, folk tales, and individual dreams.

Culture-and-personality studies developed rapidly in the 1940's, and many anthropologists began to use personality tests in the course of field work among the American Indians, peoples of the South Sea Islands, and other parts of the world. Interest also developed concerning mental illness and types of "abnormality" in primitive societies. All of these studies express a strong, continuing interrelationship between anthropological and psychological theories of human behavior.

Another reaction to the piecemeal cataloguing of customs and complexes developed into what have been called "configurational studies." Ruth Benedict's *Patterns of Culture* (1934) is the best-known expression of this trend. Taking the Pueblo Indians of the Southwest, the Kwakiutl of British Columbia, and the Dobu of the South Pacific for her main examples, she attempted to demonstrate that each culture is not just a random collection of customs haphazardly "borrowed" or diffused from surrounding cultures. Each culture, she maintained, is organized around some central configuration of ideas. Among the Pueblos it is an "Apollonian" moderation and restraint in all things, adherence to the golden mean; Kwakiutl culture, on the other hand, is supposedly pervaded by individualistic, megalomaniacal competition for prestige and honor; while Dobuan culture is characterized by a paranoid, sorcery-ridden hostility of all against all. In each case, the economy, kinship patterns, religious practices, and other major elements of custom are all thought to be shaped and interrelated by the one dominant motif.

Many anthropologists feel that Benedict's configurations were too simple and could only be maintained by ignoring much contrary evidence. M. E. Opler advanced the idea of "themes" of culture. Using Apache culture as an example, he suggested that a system of several elemental themes, rather than a single configuration, better expresses the organization of a given culture. Other anthropologists, particularly in postwar times, have developed the study of cultural values and postulates in similar attempts to describe the thematic interrelatedness of human cultural systems.

FUNCTIONALIST ANTHROPOLOGY

The main lines of anthropology in both America and Europe have come to be influenced increasingly by the so-called structural-functional school of social theory. Several writers in the nineteenth century, including Herbert Spencer, Fustel de Coulanges, and August Comte, developed theories of human social behavior that likened societies to organisms, in which the parts—the institutions, or custom complexes of the society—function to maintain the life of the society.

Following their example, Emile Durkheim, the French scholar, set forth a theory of the origins and functions of religion. He amassed evidence to show that in Australian totemic practices each social group, clan, or other kin group worships a particular totemic animal, or other natural phenomenon, and in so doing such groups are really worshipping themselves; the totemic animal or plant seems to be a symbol of the social group itself. Durkheim concluded:

> In a general way, it is unquestionable that a society has all that is necessary to arouse the sensation of the divine in minds, merely by the power that it has over them; for to its members it is what a god is to his worshippers . . . religious force is nothing other than the collective and anonymous force of the clan . . .[13]

His studies of other human institutions and customs also dwell heavily on the way these customs contribute to the maintenance of society.

Durkheim's writings strongly influenced A. R. Radcliffe-Brown, a British anthropologist who had done field work among the Andaman Islanders off the east coast of India. Radcliffe-Brown became a leading figure in British social anthropology during the period before and after World War II, and his influence is still strongly felt. He shares the limelight in functional studies with another famous anthropologist, Polish-born Bronislaw Malinowski.

Malinowski had done his doctoral work in mathematics and had also studied physics and chemistry. While on a rest from his studies, he read Frazer's *Golden Bough* and was inspired to study anthropology. After a period of study in London, he went to the Trobriand Islands, off the coast of New Guinea, and spent the entire duration of World War I (four years) engaged in research on the language, social organization, religion, economic practices, and nearly every other aspect of the Trobriand way of life. Very few field workers have so thoroughly immersed themselves in the daily lives of a people for purposes of anthropological study.

The Trobriand Islanders, like the Lycians described by Herodotus, are matrilineal in kinship organization, and Malinowski realized that they constituted a crucial test of Freud's Oedipus complex theory. According to Freud's view, all peoples everywhere

---

[13]*The Elementary Forms of the Religious Life,* trans. Joseph Ward Swain (New York: Collier Books, 1961), pp. 236 ff.

are supposed to experience the Oedipal problem: the management of aggression toward one's father because of sexual jealousies concerning one's mother, accompanied by suppressed sexual longing for the mother. Among the matrilineal Trobrianders, however, Malinowski found that a growing boy's hostilities are directed at his maternal uncle, because that uncle is the person who has authority over the boy and trains him for adult life. The Trobriand boy's father is a friendly, helpful person, and exercises little or no authority over his son. Also, Malinowski found that sexual guilt over forbidden desires involved not the mother, but the sister; thus the ethnographic data from the matrilineal Trobrianders suggested that sharp revision was needed in Freudian psychological theory.

As Malinowski wrote and published more of his Trobriand Islands materials, a new theoretical framework took shape. To him, cultural practices make up a tightly interrelated network, the whole of which is to be understood in terms of relationships to the psychobiological needs of individuals in society. While Durkheim and Radcliffe-Brown interpreted magic and religion as serving the needs of *societies* as organisms, Malinowski pointed to the way in which these practices and beliefs can be understood as responses to the needs of the *individual* human organism.

For example, Malinowski noted that the Trobriand Islanders (and their neighbors) do not use magic in seagoing operations that are safe and sound, near shore. For such ventures their canoe-building and sailing techniques are perfectly adequate. But when they must sail farther out, where sudden storms or other unforeseen events can overtake the sailor and render useless all knowledge, skills, and techniques—where a man's life is in the hands of powers beyond the reach of his "science"—there the individual experiences helpless anxiety. Magical acts are performances that function to relieve such anxiety.

The "functionalist school" of anthropology has thus developed two differing theoretical tendencies. Malinowskian functional interpretation often emphasizes the supposed needs of individuals, while followers of Durkheim and Radcliffe-Brown stress the supposed needs of a social system. Both types of functionalism developed a strong bias against historical studies, for they attempted analysis of a socio-cultural system operating at a given point in time. Functionalist theory has led to great improvements in field research, since analysis of the functional importance of particular customs and institutions often leads to more thorough and systematic gathering of information than does simple cataloguing of customs.

POSTWAR DEVELOPMENTS IN ANTHROPOLOGICAL THOUGHT

From the foregoing we see that, by the beginning of World War II, the Boasian "anti-evolutionist" school of anthropology had experienced sharp modifications. From a number of points of view the individual, the acting person and his psychological characteristics, has been reintroduced into general theorizing about the nature of human behavioral patterns. More and more, culture and society are both looked on as systems, functionally interwoven structures, rather than as simply agglomerations or lists of cultural customs and institutions.

A more sober appraisal of culture history led many anthropologists to admit that there were germs of truth, after all, in many of the ideas of Morgan and Tylor and other nineteenth-century "armchair theorists"; in fact, at least one anthropologist (Leslie White) has taken the position that Lewis Henry Morgan was a great thinker whose signal contributions to anthropology had been entirely, almost maliciously, misrepresented by the Boasians and other later anthropologists. White and his followers have built up a massive array of materials and arguments reinterpreting Morgan's evolutionist ideas in a new light, strongly colored by their "energy theory" of culture. In this view, cultural development is the result of changes in amounts of energy available to societies, influenced by the type of technology used to utilize the energy sources.

During World War II, anthropologists were called upon to make their special knowledge helpful to the U.S. and Allied cause. Anthropologists reshaped ethnographic information into manuals and handbooks about New Guinea, the peoples of Southeast Asia, survival in the jungle and desert, and how to win the affections of hostile natives. Other anthropologists studied the cultural characteristics of major nations—both enemy and ally—to provide information for military decisions as well as for handbooks on how to understand the British. Ruth Benedict's *Chrysanthemum and the*

Sword, concerning the Japanese national culture, is one of the best known of these wartime products.

When the war was over, anthropologists were called in as "trouble-shooters" in the administration of island communities in the South Pacific. They had the dual job of interpreting administrative policies to the natives and trying to explain native customs and reactions to administrators. Often the anthropological knowledge was helpful, but difficulties arose because of differences in points of view between administrator and anthropologist. Homer G. Barnett has described some of these problems in his book, *Anthropology and Administration.*

The Society for Applied Anthropology had been founded in 1941, and the pages of its journal, *Human Organization,* now carry a variety of articles concerning anthropological study of mental hospitals, community development programs in Latin America, and many other applied programs. India has been the scene of particularly intense activities, and anthropologists have found themselves coping with problems of introduction of new medical practices, new crops and agricultural techniques, and many other practical problems.

Other tendencies that mark current anthropological studies are:

Increased interest in study of complex modern societies, including community studies in Japan, Europe, Mexico, and inside the United States.

Increased co-operation with sociologists, psychologists, geographers, and scholars in related fields.

Increased interrelating of historical, functionalist, biological, psychological, and even evolutionist concepts into a unified theory of human behavior.

In this review of the history of anthropology it appears that one can roughly (and arbitrarily) divide the succession of recent events into (approximately) fifty-year periods: 1850 to 1900 marks the rise and decline of evolutionism; 1900 to 1945 may be regarded as the "Boasian" or "culture historical" period (Boas died in 1942); and the end of World War II marks the beginning of new developments in anthropology. We can only guess at the outlines of the anthropology that will characterize the final decades of the twentieth century.

Suggested Reading

*Hays, H. R. *From Ape to Angel: An Informal History of Social Anthropology.* New York: G. P. Putnam's Sons, 1964.

This well-illustrated book treats the reader to casual glimpses into the personal lives and research efforts of Morgan, Tylor, Boas, Frazer, and a long list of other eminent anthropologists.

*Kardiner, Abram, and Edward Preble. *They Studied Man.* Mentor Books edition; New York: New American Library of World Literature, Inc., 1963.

These authors discuss the lives and works of a selected group of scholars, working up from Morgan and Tylor to Sigmund Freud and Abram Kardiner in order to highlight the strong interrelations that have grown up between psychoanalysis and anthropology.

Advanced Reading

Bunzel, Ruth, and Margaret Mead. *The Golden Age of American Anthropology.* New York: George Braziller, Inc., 1960.

This is a collection of colorful writings from the early days of anthropology, mainly illustrating nineteenth- and early twentieth-century ethnographic reporting on the American Indians.

Penniman, T. K. *One Hundred Years of Anthropology* (2nd ed.). London: Gerald Duckworth and Co., Ltd., 1952.

The British have a somewhat different view of the definition and scope of anthropology, and this book is a useful supplement to our version of the history of anthropology.

---

* Paperback.

chapter three

Methods of Anthropological Research

The field of anthropology may be looked on as a "subculture," with its own social organization, customs, values, and ways of doing things. In this chapter we shall examine briefly the "customs" and procedures that anthropologists employ in the search for information about the nature of man.

Field work is undoubtedly the favorite activity of anthropologists, for research in all the subfields of anthropology is frequently pursued in out-of-the-way places, distant lands—in Africa, the Arctic, or the South Pacific. An anthropologist's first field trip—particularly if it deals with a primitive society, far from cities and civilization—is regarded as an initiation rite after which he is "never the same again." It can truthfully be said that those few anthropologists who have concentrated on library research and avoided the risks and rigors of field work are looked down on by the rest of the profession.

The romantic aura around field work sometimes obscures the fact that the anthropologist collects information in the field for later painstaking work at home—in the laboratory and the library. For every month spent in Africa, the South Seas, or the jungles of New Guinea, the anthropologist usually spends many months analyzing and writing up his findings.

ARCHAEOLOGY

Nearly everyone who has watched adventure shows on television or has read one of the many accounts of finding lost cities or ancient treasures has some ideas about the methods of archaeological research. The idea of digging recurs over and over in our mental image of the archaeologist, and the field project of an archaeologist is often referred to as a "dig."

What is not generally known, however, is the highly developed pattern of techniques the archaeologist employs in accomplishing his field-work objectives.

1. Meticulous care is taken that excavated materials are not damaged in the process of digging.

2. The position and context of every object excavated is recorded by a combination of drawings, notes, and photographs so that the archaeologist can later establish with great accuracy which items found in an excavation belong together in a particular complex of materials for a particular time period, as represented, for example, in the levels of deposited materials—the stratigraphy—of a given site.

3. All significant associated items are collected and recorded: soil samples, remains of animal and vegetable materials, types of rocks and other geological specimens, and all kinds of other materials associated with the monuments, buildings, burial goods, jewels, artwork, stone tools, weapons, or other human handiwork that the archaeologist uncovers.

Well-financed amateur archaeologists who report amazing finds of "lost cities," "fantastic works of art," and "untranslated inscriptions" are often found to be despoilers of archaeological materials because they do *not* attend carefully to the major requirements of mapping and recording mentioned above. When an archaeological find is dug up carelessly, there is usually no way to go about establishing the time sequences of materials, the relationships of various objects to one another, and other information crucial to scientific study. In a way, the archaeologist is something like a detective, for the clues he searches for are often extremely subtle.

In order to carry out the preserving of data and materials, the archaeologist often must bring a portable laboratory to his field-work location. Having set up his equipment at an archaeological site (often the selection of the site itself is the result of months of painstaking exploration and surveying), the archaeologist maps out the main outlines within which he will work. The places to be excavated are divided into carefully measured tracts—perhaps four-foot squares, for example, and each digger goes to work in a particular tract, exercising great care not to damage any materials he unearths. When the archaeologist finds any significant object—a tool, a skeleton, a scrap of a work of art—he uncovers it very slowly, sometimes using such fine tools as dental picks, toothbrushes, and small paint brushes in order to avoid damaging delicate materials. Without special training in these techniques, a digger would break up and ruin many of the objects discovered.

When the archaeologist has his thousands and thousands of items excavated, marked, recorded, classified, and shipped safely back to his home laboratory, the field-work stage of his research is over and the hard work of scientific analysis begins in earnest. (Once again, the mark-of the *amateur* archaeologist is that he often contents himself with the exhilaration of exhibition and description of what he found in the field work, without going into the hard work of analysis that would convert his results into useful scientific knowledge.)

Dating Archaeological Remains

A major methodological problem that faces the archaeologist is the matter of chronology—establishing time periods and sequences for materials that have no written evidence of dates attached to them. Archaeological publications are full of time charts of cultural materials—put together from pieces of information gleaned from hundreds of different excavations. Some of the major methods of establishing sequences and dates for archaeological materials include:

Stratigraphic evidence. If an archaeological site is relatively undisturbed, it often can be assumed that materials found close to the surface are newer or younger than materials found deep in the ground.

Association with plant and animal remains. For example, flint handaxes found with the bones of long-extinct types of elephants, mammoths, and other animals, are among the important chronological clues for early man in Western Europe. Similarly, the bones of extinct forms of camels, horses, and bison found with Indian artifacts help to establish relative ages of some North American archaeological remains.

Pollen analysis. Pollen grains found in association with archaeological finds may tell the archaeologist what kinds of plants grew in the area at the time the materials were left on the ground. Particular combinations of plants may have been characteristic of the area at only certain time periods in the past.

Dendrochronology (tree-ring dating). Annual tree-rings display variable patterns of spacing, depending on the wetness or dryness of particular years. Each sequence of years forms a unique pattern of rings. Many of the rich archaeological remains in Arizona and New Mexico have been dated by systematic tree-ring analysis of the timbers found in the sites.

Calendar dating. Some advanced civilizations, such as that of the Maya in Middle America and the Egyptian and Sumerian in the Old World, had calendrical systems, and dates of some archaeological materials may be interpolated from carved inscriptions. The big problem for the archaeologist is often the deciphering and analysis of the calendrical systems.

Cross-dating from other cultural materials. Sometimes archaeological sites in Europe have coins included in them for which nearly exact dates are obtainable. This establishes that the site *cannot be older* than those dated coins, but it may be younger.

Association with extinct shorelines and other geological features. In northern Europe, where the Finnish and Scandinavian lands continue to rise out of the sea at a relatively constant rate, archaeological finds that were originally at the seashore, or at the edge of a lake, can be dated by calculation of the approximate number of hundreds of years it has taken for that shoreline to rise so far from the water. A striking case of this sort is a series of rock carvings on a cliff in northern Norway which could only have been reached by boat. Since the carvings are now a number of feet above sea level, it is estimated that the works of art are several thousands of years old.

Radiological dating. Radiocarbon dating is one of the most striking scientific developments affecting archaeological work in recent years. This method depends on the fact that plants and animals contain a fixed amount of a radioactive isotope of carbon, called C_{14}, which deteriorates after death at a constant rate, leaving ordinary carbon (C_{12}).

By measuring the amount of C_{14} radioactivity remaining in a particular specimen, archaeologists can obtain an estimated date for that specimen and the materials associated with it. This method of dating puts the entire problem of archaeological dating on a much firmer footing. Gathering the materials (charcoal, wood, and plant fibers are preferred) for radiocarbon analysis requires great care by the archaeologist to insure that the materials are not contaminated by contact with other things that would affect the C_{14} count of the sample.

Since most of the measurable radioactive carbon is gone from a given sample after about 45,000 years, this method of dating is not useful for remains older than that figure. Archaeologists hope very much that physicists will discover other kinds of radioactive materials for accurate dating of objects in the range of 50,000 to 1,000,000 years old.

The dating of materials occupies an important place in our discussion because so much archaeological analysis depends on first establishing the ages of various sites and materials relative to one another. When the archaeologist has established some dates for his materials, his task is only begun, however. The modern archaeologist is interested in inferring general social and cultural facts from the material objects left in the ground. For example, if he excavates a small village and finds that all the house remains are alike except for one that is much larger, richer, and better furnished, he may be led to infer that the larger house represents the dwelling of a chief. On the other hand, if the unusual house floor has numbers of ritual objects in it, it may be suggested that the special occupant was a religious leader. Complex inferences from archaeological remains allow the archaeologist to speak of growth of empires, overthrow of dynasties, development of a middle class, spread of new religions, increasing craft specialization, victories and defeats in warfare, and other important social events. It is easy to see, then, why the archaeologist can make a significant contribution to history, as well as to other fields of study.

PHYSICAL ANTHROPOLOGY

"Digging up old skeletons" is the usual stereotype of field work in physical anthropology, and this is still an important part of that branch of study. One culture hero among physical anthropologists, Dr. L. S. B. Leakey, has spent a large portion of his adult life in searching for human fossil remains in East Africa. His recent finds of human remains dating possibly from nearly two million years ago are the fruits of many years of field work. Much of the field work of the physical anthropologist takes the same patterns, digging for and dating remains, that were described for the archaeologist. In fact, they often work together. The main difference between the two areas of study is that the archaeologist seeks information concerning man's culture history, while the physical anthropologist searches for evidence of man's biological evolution.

Physical anthropologists also carry out field research on living human communities. In the past this activity often consisted of obtaining measurements of peoples' height, weight, eye color, hair texture and color, and—most important of all—the cephalic index, or skull measurement. The cephalic index, obtained by dividing the width of the skull by its length, was formerly thought to be a very important clue to relationships among the different populations, or "races" of people. More recent investigations have shown, however, that the supposedly fixed and reliable cephalic index can be strongly affected by environment. Some populations that were thought to be long-headed have in some mysterious way become more round-headed, forcing abandonment of that means of "racial" classification.

New, revolutionary developments in physical anthropology have produced greatly refined methods of measurement and observation of human physical types. Increasingly, the physical anthropologists are concerned with *internal* characteristics of the human body—components of the blood and other body fluids, measures of body fat (obtained by examining skin folds and through X rays), blood pressures, growth rates, and many other complex characteristics of people. Analysis of blood types has been particularly important in recent years, for it has been found that the A-B-O blood types, and the other, lesser-known components of blood, are excellent clues to genetic inheritance.

LINGUISTICS

Nineteenth-century linguists had very little equipment to aid them in field work. Having arrived in the community in which he intended to study a particular language, the linguist located an informant (someone willing and able to speak to the linguist in the local tongue) and asked him to say particular words and sentences. The linguist simply relied on his own ears to pick up the sounds of the language, which he transcribed into his notebooks in the form of phonetic markings—the linguists' own special cross-cultural alphabet. Very often, of course, the linguist also needed an interpreter to help him, unless his informants were bilingual.

The linguist frequently collects his information on language in the form of stories—folk tales, myths, and so on, so that the professional linguist may be a collector of folklore as well.

Thomas Alva Edison's phonograph (patented in 1877) produced a major revolution in the field methods of linguists. The year after the phonograph was available to the public, the anthropologist J. W. Fewkes used one to collect forty cylinders of sample vocabularies, folklore texts, conversations, and other materials from the Passamaquoddy Indians in Maine. For the first time, the sounds of

the native speaker—his own intonations and speech patterns—
could be stored away to be played back later as the linguist analyzed
his data.

The nineteenth-century linguist generally analyzed languages
by analogy with the categories of Latin, the language of scholars.
Description of a previously unstudied language involved the search
for nouns, adjectives, prepositions, prefixes, suffixes, and other
familiar elements of grammar. It was Franz Boas and his students
who broke away from the narrow view of Latin grammatical categories and concentrated on description of American Indian languages in terms of their own "natural" grammatical elements.

Linguists have found that each language is a self-contained and
unique system for categorizing and talking about experience; some
languages do not even have words in the way we ordinarily think
of the word *word*. The Eskimo language, for example, expresses
ideas such as "The man stood on the high hill" in complex clusters
of "idea particles" or morphemes, which cannot be separated out
into six or seven words, as in the English sentence, but rather are
all stuck together into a single "word-sentence."

Although linguists try to describe individual languages in terms
of their own intrinsic patterns of grammar and sounds, they make
systematic comparisons among languages, searching for "families
of languages" descended from common ancestors. As mentioned
earlier, the discovery that most of the languages in Europe are
all descended from a common ancestral proto-Indo-European
language was one of the great revolutionary developments of
linguistics. Related languages are discovered by systematic comparison of their vocabularies for sound-and-meaning correspond-
ences. For example, if *hound* in English refers to a kind of dog, and
hund in German also refers to man's best friend, then it is probable
that both words are derived from a common ancestral form. Systematic comparison of large numbers of such English-German word
pairs provides the evidence that the two languages are related. The
linguist's comparative method becomes quite complicated by the
fact that all languages change in pronunciation and grammar over
the years and centuries. The similarities between German and
English are relatively easy to spot, but it is harder to understand
how, for example, the Russian word pronounced *adyin* is related to
our English word *one*.

The research methods of the linguist, like those of other anthropologists, have been greatly assisted by modern mechanical devices
such as magnetic recorders, sound spectrographs, and electronic

computers, but none of these machines make any less complex the painstaking analysis that the researcher must carry out with his own brain, eyes, and hands.

THE METHODS OF SOCIAL ANTHROPOLOGY

The cultural (social) anthropologist gathers his raw materials by means of field work in primitive or not-so-primitive communities, where he usually lives for several months. (Many current field studies last over a year.) He attempts to observe as much as possible of the ways of life of the people he is studying. There are many recent innovations in field-work techniques, but the old and the new methods of field work that the anthropologist uses are variations around two major procedures: 1) interviewing of informants, and 2) participant observation.

Like the linguist, the social anthropologist seeks out reliable, knowledgeable informants—those people in the community who know the most about the life of the community, and are the most willing to tell what they know. In some communities nearly everyone is willing to tell a lot about the local way of life; in other places the anthropologist must work hard to establish enough trust so that even one or two people will consent to give extensive information. Again, like the linguist, the anthropologist must often hire an interpreter, unless he has learned the local language beforehand. Nowadays, of course, in increasing numbers of societies there are highly capable bilinguals whose second language is English or French or Spanish. But most anthropologists seek to learn the local language during their field-work period—even if field work is possible in the anthropologist's own language. The reasons for the anthropologist's interest in language are threefold: 1) most people in primitive and folk communities feel increasing closeness and trust toward those outsiders who make an attempt to learn their language; 2) the anthropologist who does not speak the local language misses much information because he does not understand conversations going on around him; 3) frequently the social meanings of particular elements of human behavior are poorly expressed in translated form, and the anthropologist cannot get an adequate understanding of them until he has full descriptions in the native tongue.

The experiences of anthropologists and others have taught us over the years that even in a small community any one informant does not know all about life in that community, nor is he always accurate in telling what he knows. Any informant in a small town probably knows how many policemen and doctors there are. Most informants know which local stores have what commodities. But few informants can be uniformly reliable in matters of what towns-people eat for supper, what they think about outsiders, where people go for medical care, and other complex human affairs. Therefore, the anthropologist tries to locate and use the services of a number of different informants who occupy diverse positions in the local community. He tries to interview individuals from different family groups, different neighborhoods, different social classes, and other major sub-units of the local society. The information given by these various persons can be cross-checked for accuracy. Often the upper-class members of a village are not well informed on the details of behavior of lower-class individuals, and vice versa.

Even the best informants, cross-checked against one another, provide the anthropologist with a very distilled, inadequate picture of life in a society. A native might be completely unconscious of, or take for granted, and thus not mention, aspects of his culture that would have great significance to the outside observer. Much of the richness of information the anthropologist wants from the tribe or village or band that he is studying can be obtained only by "participant observation"—the participation by the anthropologist in the activities themselves. The anthropologist hopes to be so accepted in the regular life of the community that he can be present and take part in hunting activities, planting of crops, religious ceremonies, initiation rites, weddings and wakes, as well as the day-to-day routines of social interaction—visiting, gossiping, games, and other recreation in the community.

As participant observer the anthropologist tries to accomplish several major objectives. First, he hopes that by being involved rather extensively in the local life, he can gain the respect and trust of the local people, so that they will feel confidence in him and willingly reveal to him aspects of their private lives. Second, participation is often the best way to see the complex details of human behavior. A Pueblo rainmaking ceremony, for example, cannot be fully described by an informant, however eloquent he may be. It has to be seen by the anthropologist for himself. Having seen the ceremony, he can then ask intelligent questions about it, for fuller understanding. Third, the anthropologist often finds that the *emotional* meaning of a particular human activity does not become clear to him until he has experienced the activity himself. The anthropologist, thus, is an investigator who wants to find out how it "feels" to take part in an arduous hunting expedition, to dance all night in a harvest festival, or to sit in a darkened room watching and listening to the performance of a gifted "shaman" or medicine man as he cures a sick person.

In this writer's field work among Lappish people in northeastern Finland, the complexities, the excitement, and the subtle interaction of men and animals in the reindeer roundup came clear only after he had actually worked in the corral trying to rope some of the elusive animals.

THE PATTERNING OF BEHAVIOR

Anthropologists frequently point out that the ways of life of a given people contain many customs or patterns of behavior that are highly predictable, highly regular, so that no statistical count is necessary to substantiate the generalizations made by the anthropologist. Such highly regular patterning of behavior is most clearly seen in language. We do not need to study a large sample of informants in order to find out what the past tense of the verb *run* is supposed to be. The logic of patterning (the rules) of language is such that nearly all English speakers agree on the use of the term *ran* as the past tense. In simple societies, the anthropologist argues, many items of behavior and belief are similarly governed by uniform rules. In fact, the rules of any language can be looked on as simply a particularly clear instance of the generalization that human social behavior in every society follows regular rules—customs, mores, standards, for different situations—that are learned by individuals as they grow up in their particular societies. The main details of the handling of boats, throwing of the nets, and hauling in of fish are likely to be very much the same for each group of fishermen in an Eskimo fishing village. It is not necessary for the anthropologist to take a poll of the fishermen to describe the chief elements of these activities.

This regular patterning of behavior in all human societies makes it possible for the individuals in each community to predict one another's behavior and interact for mutual satisfaction of interests. Even fights and warfare are carried out according to "rules" and customs. How angry the British redcoats were when they found that the American Revolutionists didn't behave according to accepted European customs of military behavior!

But recognition of the patterning of behavior has sometimes led anthropologists and others to give the impression that primitive and folk societies are slaves of custom and tradition, with little variation in behavior within local communities. Those individuals in primitive societies who seemed to vary from the dead level of average behavior have often been labeled "deviant" or "exceptional," thus preserving the illusion that most of the people in the tribe or village were pretty much alike.

THE ANTHROPOLOGIST AS "RESEARCH INSTRUMENT"

Social anthropologists have sometimes written their reports and books on primitive communities with a cavalier disregard for presentation of the evidence used to arrive at general conclusions. Some anthropologists have maintained that their generalizations about the personality, the emotional tone, the ethos of a particular way of life cannot be demonstrated objectively with systematic evidence. The reader must, in effect, trust to the honesty and objectivity of the anthropologist, much as the judgment of a work of art must be left to individual subjective experience.

This subjective element in anthropological field work has been under heavy attack. Critics have pointed out, for example, that earlier anthropologists, notably Ruth Benedict, described the Zuni and other Pueblo Indian ways of life as harmonious, moderate, peaceful—idyllic in every way imaginable. Later investigators, however, have accumulated evidence that these same Pueblo peoples are anxiety-ridden and quick to suspect and accuse one another of witchcraft. Given these discrepancies in reports by anthropologists on the Pueblo peoples, one might wonder whether there is anything about anthropological field work that is trustworthy.

Psychologists, sociologists, and others who expect almost all research information to be accompanied by statistical tables with appropriate calculations of averages and probabilities, point out that anthropological descriptions usually do not tell how many informants state a particular generalization; and all too often the anthropologist does not describe what individual behavior or statements led him to a particular generalization about the customs of a given people. Anthropologists have, at times, been somewhat careless, even secretive, about the nature of their field-work observations.

Facing up to these serious criticisms has resulted in a great deal of soul-searching and controversy within the ranks of anthropologists. Many of the criticisms concerning subjectivity and carelessness with evidence have been accepted as valid complaints, and anthropologists have searched for ways to overcome subjectivity in their methods. At the same time, they have tried to preserve those elements of anthropological method which were felt to be crucial to the scholarly tasks that anthropologists set for themselves.

In some areas of study, anthropologists have adopted the empirical techniques—particularly various tests—of other social scientists. In her study of the Alorese, mentioned earlier, Dr. Cora DuBois made extensive use of Rorschach projective tests, life histories, dreams of individuals, and analyses of drawings, in addition to gathering standard ethnographic data. She submitted the psychological materials to analysis by specialists, who interpreted the tests "blind"—that is, without knowledge of the cultural materials collected by the anthropologist.[1]

Other anthropological studies have introduced use of questionnaire schedules and careful sampling procedures borrowed from the methods of sociology (often in joint projects involving both sociologists and anthropologists). A comparative study of value orientations among the Zuni and Navaho Indians, Mormons, "Texans," and Spanish-Americans was undertaken in the southwestern United States by a team of anthropologists and sociologists.[2] A questionnaire was prepared, involving a series of situations, such as the following:

A man had a crop failure, or let us say, had lost most of his sheep or cattle. He and his family had to have help from someone if they were going to get through the winter. There are different ways of getting help. Which of these three ways would be best?

The three alternative answers posed for this question were supposed to indicate whether the respondent would 1) depend mostly on brothers and sisters and other relatives for help; 2) go to sources outside the local community for aid; or 3) turn for help to older important relatives or other local leaders who are used to managing things in his group.

Responses to the questions were collected from a sample of individuals in each of the five communities studied. These results were then carefully tabulated and analyzed statistically.

[1] *The People of Alor*, 2 vols. (paperback edition; New York: Harper and Row, 1960).

[2] Florence Kluckhohn and Fred Strodtbeck (eds.), *Variations in Value Orientations* (New York: Harper and Row, 1961).

In general, modern anthropological research shows increasing care in the presentation of evidence that can be independently examined and evaluated by other researchers.

SYNTHESIS OF ANTHROPOLOGICAL DATA

The heightened sophistication of anthropological field workers and the search for more objective research tools such as psychological tests, survey questionnaires, accurate censuses, and other techniques have greatly increased the usefulness of ethnographic reports brought back from the field. More and more, however, attention has shifted from problems of accurate reporting to the search for more accurate and useful historical and scientific generalizations from the information now available from hundreds of societies.

One important development of the past fifteen years is the growth of the cross-cultural (statistical) method for examining anthropological generalizations. Some anthropologists attempted cross-cultural studies decades ago, but this type of study has only recently begun to demonstrate its usefulness. Reasons for this success would appear to lie in the greatly increased numbers and quality of primary ethnographic reports, greater sophistication in formulation of questions for theoretical research, and improved methods of rapid collating of information, including use of electronic computers.

Until about fifteen years ago, any anthropologist who wanted to find out some piece of information from a sample of, say, sixty societies around the world, would have to read the individual field reports—the books, monographs, and research papers—on all the tribes in his sample. After laboriously searching through these individual works, he might still learn that much of the information he needed was missing. Since World War II, largely due to the efforts of Dr. George P. Murdock and his associates, the *Human Relations Area Files* (HRAF) have been established, in which information from hundreds of societies, from all the culture areas of the world, has been abstracted and assembled onto cards which are filed according to a master indexing system. For example, anyone wishing to find information on types of games played in societies around the world can go to the files, locate the appropriate index number, and gather together the required information in a fraction of the time it would have taken him to go to the original ethnographic sources. The HRAF files are now available at a number of the major universities in the United States.

A study by John W. M. Whiting and Irvin L. Child[3] offers a clear example of the cross-cultural method of anthropological study, making use of the HRAF files. The investigators were interested in examining the supposed influence of child training practices on adult customs in human societies. Using some ideas from Freudian psychoanalytic theory, modified by concepts from psychological learning theory, they hypothesized, for example, that in societies in which children are weaned early or harshly there is development of anxiety over oral activities that continues to be part of the personalities of the adults in the given society. Such anxiety about oral activities, they further reasoned, would lead to development of explanations of illnesses which emphasize oral activities—poison in one's food, eating the wrong kind of foods, and so on. To test this hypothesis (and a large number of similar hypotheses) Whiting and Child chose a sample of societies from the cross-cultural files and rated each society with respect to charac-teristics such as "severity of oral training" in childhood and also "oral explanations of illness."

The ratings of the researchers were then analyzed statistically. The results shown in Table 2 indicate support for the hypothesis that there is a relationship between the child training practice and customs concerning explanation of illness. A statistical calculation of probability for the results shown in Table 2 indicates that the striking relationships obtained (the clustering in cells B and C as compared with cells A and D) would happen by "sheer accident" less than 5 times in 10,000 attempts.

Many of the hypotheses tested by Whiting and Child did not yield results as striking as this one concerning oral anxiety, but in general their work lends support for the proposition that dif-ferences in child training practices are related to differences in adult customs. Other similarly organized studies have examined cross-cultural differences in drinking behavior, in use of "love magic," in beliefs in the helpfulness of deities, in types of kinship systems, and many other important questions.

Many anthropologists object to cross-cultural statistical studies, saying that such use of the ethnographic data removes the infor-

---

[3] *Child Training and Personality* (paperback edition; New Haven: Yale University, 1962).

TABLE 2

Relationship Between Oral Socialization Anxiety and Oral Explanations of Illness[4]

	Societies with oral explanations absent	*Societies with oral explanations present*	
	A	B	
Societies above average (median) on oral socialization anxiety	Lapps Chamorro Samoans	Marquesans Dobuans Baiga Kwoma Thonga Alorese Chagga Navaho Dahomeans	Lesu Masai Lepcha Maori Pukapukans Trobrianders Kwakiutl Manus
	C	D	
Societies below average (median) on oral socialization anxiety	Arapesh Balinese Hopi Tanala Paiute Chenchu Teton Papago Flathead Venda Warrau Wogeo Ontong-Javanese	Chiricahua Comanche Siriono Bena Slave Kurtatchi	

mation too far from the behavioral context in which it occurs, making such information unreal, abstractified, or even downright false. Supporters of the method generally admit to weaknesses in the procedure, particularly in the availability and interpretation of the raw ethnographic reports, but feel that these cross-cultural studies test particular hypotheses that can be further studied by more intensive means in individual societies.

---

[4] *Ibid.*, p. 156.

SUMMARY AND CONCLUSIONS

In all phases of anthropological research there has been a great increase in the use of technical equipment: recording devices, complex photography, X-ray devices, sound spectrographs, and electronic computers. In the non-mechanized procedures of gathering data—in interviewing, "observing-while-participating," and digging—anthropologists have become much more sensitive to the necessity for rigorous, accurate description of the observations that lie back of ethnographic generalizations. There has been a great increase in use of statistics in the analysis of certain kinds of anthropological data. Generalizations that used to be regarded as unquestioned facts have been re-examined. Anthropology has become, in many respects, more scientifically "respectable." It is probable that anthropology will continue to combine some of the descriptive, holistic methods of the humanities with the more analytic and statistically-oriented practices of the social sciences.

Suggested Reading

*Malinowski, Bronislaw. *Argonauts of the Western Pacific*. New York: E. P. Dutton and Co., Inc., 1961.

This classic ethnographic report begins with a very important discussion of anthropological field-work methods.

Advanced Reading

*Moore, Frank W. *Readings in Cross-cultural Methodology*. New Haven: Human Relations Area Files Press, 1961.

These readings illustrate significant problems in the rapidly developing area of cross-cultural studies, usually involving the Human Relations Area Files as a basic source of ethnographic data.

*Tax, Sol (ed.). *Anthropology Today—Selections*. Chicago: University of Chicago Press, 1962.

Several papers on methods of research are included in this inventory volume.

---

* Paperback.

chapter four

Significant Research in Anthropology

Few people would deny that the "study of man" is concerned with phenomena of great complexity. In fact, many critics of the social sciences have claimed that human behavior is essentially beyond effective scientific study. According to this line of argument, the influence of man's "free will," and the enormous, apparently unlimited possibilities for variations in human behavior make the efforts of generalizing about man and culture essentially fruitless, if not dangerous. To make matters worse, there is the inevitable subjectivity of man studying himself—a problem not encountered by the physical scientists in their study of atoms, animals, and astrophysics.

Critics of the social sciences (including anthropology) can point to conflicting "facts," inconsistencies in terminology, and the seemingly hopeless divergences in theoretical assumptions as evidence of the obvious immaturity of these studies. Usually skeptics point for contrast to the great precision and elaborate mathematics found in physics and chemistry. They are quick to mention advances in communications systems, in automation of industry, and, more recently, in space technology as evidence of progress in the "real sciences"—progress that they believe the social sciences can never match. In comparison with the precision achieved in firing manned rockets into space, the scientific study of man seems most chaotic and unimpressive.

Anthropology, like the other social sciences, is a rather young discipline, and every field of scholarship must pass through a relatively long stage of growing up. The formative period of a science must involve collecting of much descriptive information; trial and error testing of methods and theories (with inevitable fads or temporary explorations); organization of preliminary classifications of "types " of subjects to be studied; and many other steps. In the later "mature phase," general principles and scientific laws can be developed. Much current anthropological study is still in the data-gathering and exploratory phases. However, the gathering of descriptive information about human history and peoples of the world is no small achievement in itself, and this store of information, once gathered, can be put to a variety of uses.

THE EVIDENCE OF HUMAN EVOLUTION

Some of man's tool-using, "ape-man" ancestors may have been living in East Africa almost two million years ago.[1] A new series of fossil discoveries from Tanganyika, announced by Dr. L. S. B. Leakey in the spring of 1964, has been assigned, tentatively, an age of 1,800,000 years. Dr. Leakey has found a number of fossils in the same area, and some of the remains of these man-ape creatures were found with crude stone tools—clear evidence of human-like culture. The ages of these important "new" fossils were established by the potassium-argon method (based on the breakdown, at a constant rate, of an unusual form of potassium, which gives off the gas, argon, and leaves ordinary potassium). Leakey named his latest discovery Homo habilis ("man with ability").

In South Africa, anthropologists and their colleagues have found dozens of fossil specimens of an ape-man that has been named Australopithecus ("southern ape"). In spite of the connotations of the name, there is much evidence that this little fellow walked upright (standing about four feet tall), used bones and stones for tools, had very humanlike face and teeth, and was equipped with a brain midway between that of the ape and modern man in size. These characteristics put Australopithecus on the borderline between man and ape. So far, then, it looks as if Africa may be the "birthplace of man."

The evidence amassed during the past century concerning the biological evolution of man is truly impressive. Fossilized skulls and other skeletal remains of early man have been found in hundreds of different locations throughout the world. The first evidence of Neandertal Man, found over a hundred years ago, has been supplemented by numbers of Neandertal finds in Germany, France, Spain, Italy, Yugoslavia, and Belgium. Neandertal-like fossils have also been found in Palestine, Africa, and in Southeast Asia, suggest-

---

[1] As reported in Minneapolis Morning Tribune, Saturday, April 4, 1964.

ing a fairly wide distribution around the world for this type of early man. Neandertal Man lived about 100,000 years ago—much more recently than *Australopithecus* and *Homo habilis.*

The links between Neandertal Man and the African fossil men are a series of fossils from East Asia, particularly the famed Java Man *(Pithecanthropus erectus)* and Peking Man. The remains of Peking Man were found with fairly strong evidence of human use of fire. Geological and other methods of dating all suggest that Java Man and similar early men were living on earth about 600,000 years ago. It is important to note that sizes of the brain cases of these fossils are about halfway between that of *Australopithecus* and modern man. A most important part of human biological evolution has been the steady increase in brain size and complexity.

Fossil evidence of fully modern man—*Homo sapiens*—is abundant in Europe, Asia, and Africa. These fossils are only 10,000 to 30,000 years old. Many anthropologists argue, therefore, that *Homo sapiens* evolved in fairly recent times. On the other hand, Dr. Leakey argues that his new East African discovery, *Homo habilis,* is quite "modern" in brain size and jaw structure, suggesting that *Homo sapiens* really was nearly fully developed over a million years ago.

The fossil men and remains of their cultures that have been found in the New World—North and South America—all tell the same story. The ancestors of American Indians came from Siberia perhaps less than 50,000 years ago. There were no man-apes in the Americas.

THE EVIDENCE OF HUMAN CULTURAL EVOLUTION

For more than a million years the ancestors of man lived as small bands of hunters and foragers, using only very simple stone, bone, and wooden weapons and implements. Very few important changes occurred in the cultural equipment of man's ancestors during those first million years, as far as can be determined from archaeological research. The rich stores of stone tools that constitute our main evidence for that early period in culture history show a very gradual refinement and specialization in man's equipment, from crude pebble-tools to carefully shaped handaxes.

Archaeological excavations in Western Europe provide evidence of significant development of cultural complexity near the end of the Ice Age. During the last 40,000 years of the Great Glaciation, the "cave men" who roamed what is now France and Spain developed a style in their cave paintings and other art work that still today ranks among man's greatest artistic achievements. On the walls of nearly inaccessible underground caverns they painted amazing polychrome representations of the mammoths, bison, reindeer, and other animals that they hunted. It is generally believed that these masterworks were produced for the practical purposes of hunting magic and ritual, rather than representing *l'art pour l'art.*

The truly revolutionary changes in human culture that make our complex modern life possible developed during the past 10,000 years—a tiny fraction of man's total cultural history. The series of inventions that radically changed man's way of living was the domestication of plants and animals. Excavations by Robert Braidwood and others in Iraq, Iran, and Israel have recently given us a much better picture of the probable beginnings of the "food-production revolution." Archaeological and botanical evidence strongly favors the Near East as the probable "birthplace" of agriculture, for many of the plants that man has learned to sow, care for, and harvest grow wild in that part of the world. In some sites in the same area, archaeologists have found stone "sickles" that were probably used for harvesting the wild plants in a time before men discovered ways to plant and cultivate crops for themselves.

Braidwood and his associates have carried out systematic investigation of the site of an ancient hillside village in Iraq.[2] This village, called Jarmo, appears to have been a cluster of about twenty-five mud houses. The people who lived there grew barley and wheat and kept some domestic animals, but also relied a great deal upon wild foods as well. These people, and people of similar ancient villages of the Near East, may have been the not-so-far-removed descendants of the world's first cultivators. From radio-carbon samples the remains of the village have been dated back about 8,500 years.

Little agricultural villages like Jarmo may have been only one or two steps removed from the hunting-and-foraging way of life, but those are mighty steps. Controlling their own food supply to a much greater degree than was possible for Stone Age hunters, these people could live in settled villages, could support a larger population, and had more leisure time. The leisure time could be used simply for loafing, but it also made possible the development of

2 Robert J. Braidwood, "The Agricultural Revolution," *Scientific American,* CCIII, No. 3 (1960), 130–52.

new kinds of craftsmanship—pottery, weaving, tool-making, and other manufacturing. Given the fairly rich areas available for cultivation in the Near East, it was only a matter of time before the agriculturalists of the little hillside villages expanded their activities into the river valleys.

The world's first cities, several of them prominently mentioned in the Old Testament, were built in the fertile valleys of the Tigris and Euphrates rivers. Tremendous archaeological work has gone into the careful uncovering of evidence about the transition from little farming villages like Jarmo to the concentration of people in cities such as Al Ubaid, out of which grew Sumerian civilization. The cities were made possible by the invention of irrigation works in the river valleys, and it appears that those earliest cities were governed by theocracies of priests who controlled secular activities of food production and handicrafts, as well as the sacred ritual activities involving man's relationship with the supernatural beings.

Evidence unearthed so far indicates that those first cities developed about 4000 B.C. The evidence also shows that around that same time a great many striking new techniques and implements were invented by the people of the Mesopotamian region. Extraction and use of metals was invented, the making of bronze from a combination of tin and copper was developed, craftsmen began to do remarkably good work in manufacture of weapons, ornaments, tools, pottery, and other goods, and the record keepers for the priestly temples began to use more and more complicated marks for keeping track of grain receipts and other transactions. The first written language and mathematics came into being. The servants of the temples also developed accurate means of keeping track of the seasons by observing the movements of heavenly bodies. Astronomy, the oldest science, came into being, and with it, the first calendars.

The inventions and discoveries of the Mesopotamians spread widely in the Old World. From the archaeological evidence it appears likely that the ancient civilizations of Egypt, India, and even China were the result of the diffusion of those strategic inventions—agriculture, metal-working, and record-keeping—from the original cradle of civilization, Mesopotamia.

At the point at which the archaeological record of man's past gradually shades into the earliest dawn of written history, anthropologists and historians are greatly dependent on one another as they try to gain fuller knowledge of the rise of civilization.

TIME (APPROX.)	OLD WORLD	NEW WORLD
Now		
		Aztec and Inca Empires Mayan Civilization
Birth of Christ		
	Rise of Greek Civilization	
2,000 B. C.		Beginnings of Mayan Towns
	Invention of Metal Working, Writing, and Many Other New Things	
4,000 B. C.	First Cities in Mesopotamia	Invention of Maize-growing
	Invention of Grain-growing in Near East	
10,000 B. C.		
	Western European Cave Art	
		First Men Arrive in New World (by way of Alaska)
	Many New Forms of Stone Tools	
100,000 B. C.	Neandertal Man	
	Handaxes Found Widely in Old World	
500,000 B. C.	Java Man and Peking Man Fossils (and many stone tools)	
1 Million B. C.	Crude Stone Tools of Man Found in Africa and in Europe	
1.7 Million B. C.	Australopithecus and Homo Habilis Found with Stone Tools at Oldavai Gorge in East Africa by Leakey	

Figure 2. The History of Human Cultural and Biological Evolution—as Read from the Anthropological Evidence (read from the bottom up).

54

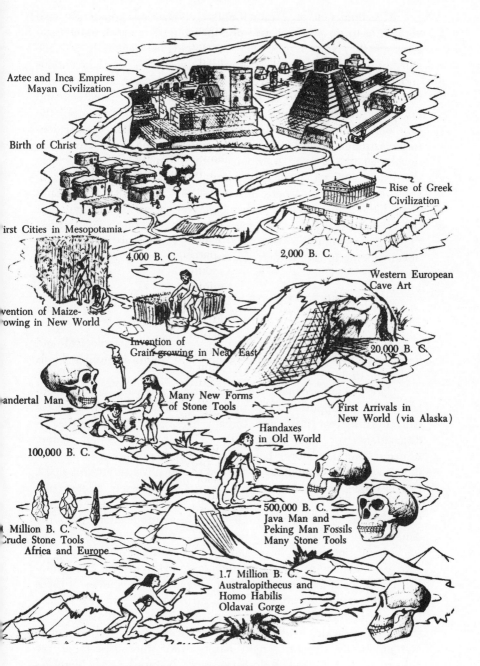

Aztec and Inca Empires
Mayan Civilization

Birth of Christ

First Cities in Mesopotamia

Rise of Greek
Civilization

4,000 B. C.

2,000 B. C.

Western European
Cave Art

Invention of Maize-
growing in New World

Invention of
Grain-growing in Near East

20,000 B. C.

Neandertal Man

Many New Forms
of Stone Tools

First Arrivals in
New World (via Alaska)

Handaxes
in Old World

100,000 B. C.

500,000 B. C.
Java Man and
Peking Man Fossils
Many Stone Tools

Million B. C.
Crude Stone Tools
Africa and Europe

1.7 Million B. C.
Australopithecus and
Homo Habilis
Oldavai Gorge

Man's Trek—as Read from the Anthropological Evidence.

55

The influence of Mesopotamian civilization apparently had very little to do with the rise of Mayan, Aztec, and Inca civilizations of the New World. The archaeological materials tell the story of an independent development, involving a set of inventions and discoveries different from those of the Near East. Quite different foods were cultivated—maize, beans, squash, tomatoes, and potatoes, all of which were unknown in the Old World until the time of Columbus; and metal-working, writing, mathematics, calendars, astronomy, and other achievements appear to have been developed out of local traditions, rather than being carried from the distant civilizations of Mesopotamia and Egypt. The remarkable achievements of the American Indians took place several thousand years later than similar growth in the Near East. In fact, much of the growth of Middle American and Peruvian (Inca) civilizations took place within the past 2,000 years. A summary of the main developments in the history of man is presented in Figure 2.

OTHER EVIDENCE CONCERNING HUMAN CULTURE HISTORY

As we approach more recent times, the archaeological and fossil evidence are supported more and more by other kinds of information.

Careful measurement and observations of living human populations lend support to the view that most of the peoples of Europe, the Near East, and India are related to one another as descendants of one branch—the Caucasoid stock—of *Homo sapiens*. The prehistoric background of other areas also can be illuminated by examination of the data from physical anthropology. For example, the American Indians are most closely related biologically to the Mongoloid peoples of Northeast Asia, adding to the weight of evidence underlying the proposition that the Americas were settled from Asia by way of the Bering Straits.

Linguistic studies have shown that most of the peoples of Europe and India speak related languages—all of the Indo-European language family. Meticulous comparative studies of these languages make possible the reconstruction of portions of the language of the Indo-European ancestor. These vocabulary reconstructions provide evidence for inferences about the economic system, family structure, food habits, and other aspects of the culture of the ancient Indo-Europeans. Naturally, the linguistic and biological data are most usually examined in conjunction with archaeological information. Careful sifting of linguistic, archaeological, and biological evidence about culture history is especially important for those parts of the world in which there has been little written history until recent times. Maps of related language groupings, the occurrence of particular complexes of cultural traits, together with archaeological evidence, have helped to reconstruct some outlines of the prehistory of Africa, the Americas, and other parts of the world. Evidence from language and culture are the main sources of information about the almost unbelievable migrations of Polynesians and related peoples throughout the islands of the South Seas. People with Malayo-Polynesian languages and related customs are found all the way from Madagascar, off the east coast of Africa, to Easter Island (which belongs to Chile) —a distance of over 13,000 miles, or more than halfway around the globe! To travel such wide spans of ocean these peoples had only their little sailing canoes.

THE DATA ON HUMAN BEHAVIOR

The masses of information that anthropologists have collected about the peoples of the world always point in two directions. Looking backward, we are naturally interested in tracing man's biological and cultural history, as outlined above. The same information, however, is also the raw material from which we seek to put together generalizations about human behavior. We want to understand modern human behavior in all its forms, rather than merely to learn some interesting facts about the past.

Now, if a biologist were searching for generalizations about the behavior of birds, it is unlikely that he would rely upon data limited to descriptions of the behavior of birds of North America. Similarly, no sensible oceanographer attempts to study the characteristics of the oceans using only information from the North Atlantic. These scientists search out the fullest possible information from all parts of our globe when pursuing study of their favorite subject. It therefore seems strange to anthropologists that there have been so many studies made and books written about human nature, religion, law, art, and other aspects of man using information from one small subgroup of humans—namely, Americans and Europeans.

The tendency of many scholars to generalize about man's ways from such a narrow sampling of the available evidence appears to be due to two main factors. First, information about the beliefs, institutions, marriage patterns, economic systems, and personalities of the great variety of non-European peoples has not been easily available to everyone. Until about 100 years ago there was no systematically collected mass of ethnographic data. The second, and perhaps more important reason, is that all men everywhere tend to view their own way of life as the most reasonable and natural—as exemplary of human behavior at its best. It is not surprising, therefore, that even the most profound philosophers of both East and West have commonly derived their theories of human nature from study of their own countrymen and neighboring nations, deeming the customs of more distant peoples as savage, quaint, barbaric, illogical, unnatural, or even subhuman.

As early as the seventeenth and eighteenth centuries, however, some European philosophers began to use information about the Red Indians and the people of the South Seas as evidence for their theories. J. J. Rousseau's use of ethnographic materials for his concept of the "noble savage" is an example of this tendency. The ethnographic information available to these men was, of course, rather scanty and inaccurate, since it had been collected in an unorganized manner by a variety of travelers, adventurers, missionaries, and others, as a sideline to their major activities and interest. The philosophers could hardly draw useful conclusions about human nature when their ethnographic sources told of one-eyed giants, tribes with mouths in the middle of their stomachs, people without either language or religion, and other fantasies.

Only in the twentieth century has the level of ethnographic information so improved that the more striking absurdities have been dropped from common belief, and something approaching accurate descriptions of human lifeways have become available from the important geographical sub-areas of the world. Even today there are great gaps in the availability of particular kinds of information. To give just one example, only since about 1945 have anthropologists made serious attempts to gather systematic data on child-rearing practices.

Widespread recognition among non-anthropologists of the importance of cross-cultural materials for generalizations about human behavior has developed only in the past twenty-five years. Almost anyone writing today on such subjects as religious systems, the human family, personality development, or law-ways, feels compelled to take notice of at least some of the rich store of relevant information from non-Western societies.

PROMISING DEVELOPMENTS IN ANTHROPOLOGICAL THEORY

The accumulation of descriptive information about human behavior, past and present, has now reached proportions which make possible significant advances in anthropological theory. One of the perennially favorite topics of anthropological theory has been the question of cultural evolution—the search for general stages or regular patterns in human culture history. After the nineteenth-century version of cultural evolution had been thoroughly discredited, most anthropologists avoided—almost as a kind of supernatural taboo—any examination of cultural evolutions. In more recent times, there have been serious attempts to build new theories on better foundations.

Julian Steward has advanced a theory that he calls "multilinear evolution." [3] Instead of assuming that human lifeways everywhere advance through similar sequences of progress from "savagery" to "civilization," Steward has searched for more limited parallels among societies developing in comparable environmental situations. Looking at the rise of civilizations in Mesopotamia, Egypt, China, Peru, and Middle America, Steward (along with other anthropologists) has noted that quite similar processes of cultural growth took place in these widely separated circumstances. The "formative period" in each of these areas was marked by development of metallurgy, population growth, expansion of the dominant culture, building of large irrigation works, and appearance of multi-community "state" organization. Steward's theories suggest that the development of complex societies in other kinds of natural environments (e.g., Northern Europe) would be expected to take different patterns from the ones just described. This theoretical framework assumes that cultural processes must be studied as an interaction among environment, social organization, technological inventory, and ideological patterns—acting upon and influencing each other as men adapt to given environments and try to improve their conditions of living.

---

[3] *Theory of Culture Change* (Urbana: University of Illinois Press, 1955).

Many of the earlier anthropological descriptions of particular peoples were presented merely as lists of the various "peculiar" customs found in the particular society, with little conception of how these customs were related to one another, or how the society practicing them was organized.

Emerging anthropological theory is based on the general postulate that different customs and behaviors within a given society are functionally interrelated. Further, anthropologists assume that any community of people can be described as organized into a social system in which individuals and groups play various parts, or "roles," in the drama of living. These basic assumptions can be employed in the study of any aspect of human cultural or social organization.

Anthropological research shows that the conjugal family—man and wife, plus children—is a fundamental unit in nearly all human societies. In addition to this core unit, however, societies differ widely in the ways and the extent to which kinship relationships are organizing principles for larger social units. Some very large tribes (especially in Africa) are politically and socially organized mainly into bodies of patrilineal kinsmen (group membership reckoned through males only); other tribes of the same size have kings and political administrations based on non-kinship relationships. Many societies that practice hoe-cultivation of crops, as in South America, Africa, and elsewhere, have matrilineal kin groups (group membership reckoned through females). Again, many of the world's peoples consider paternal and maternal kinsmen of equal importance in the formation of social groups and alliances.

As a general rule, it can be said that development of complex, industrial societies has brought an increase in the varieties of non-kinship social groupings (clubs, associations, unions, corporations, etc.). But many primitive societies also have "clubs," craft guilds, religious societies, and other groupings of non-kin; and family and kinship relations still provide the foundations for important elements of human behavior in complex modern societies.

Much anthropological research has recently gone into the examination of beliefs in magic and witchcraft. Educated representatives of our own way of life generally regard these elements of "superstition" as clear evidence of backwardness and irrationality. Missionaries, governmental agents, and others campaign against the magical beliefs and witchcraft practices of Australian aborigines, Africans, and American Indians, often without much apparent success. Usually, those who have sought to stamp out such practices have naively regarded these ideas as simply remnants of pagan beliefs—relics of the past.

As we noted in Chapter 2, it was Bronislaw Malinowski who first clearly suggested and produced evidence for the relationship between magical practices and life's areas of uncertainty.[4] Those pulse-quickening situations in hunting, warfare, ocean sailing, or other activities where a man's technical abilities are insufficient to affect the uncontrollables of weather, wild animals, stormy seas, dangerous enemies—these are the kinds of situations in which men everywhere turn to wish-projections in the form of magical practices. Malinowski saw this response to anxiety as a natural attribute of all humans, including both the Trobriand sailor on the high seas and the modern American embarking on unusually difficult action. Everyone does not incline to magical practices to the same degree, but examples from our own modern society support Malinowski's theory. In areas where our abilities and technology are in doubt—in struggles with incurable illnesses, the dangers of warfare, and even in the uncertainties of hardfought ballgames—we "moderns" easily show interest in rabbits' feet, lucky talismans of all sorts, mystical quack medicines, magical avoidance of certain words and dozens of other little rituals. Even religious conversions and visionary experiences appear related to intense anxieties. It would be very interesting to compile materials on the magical practices employed by college students at examination time—the most anxiety-ridden situation in the academic world!

In an excellent study of two West African societies, S. F. Nadel has demonstrated that accusations of witchcraft tend to be leveled at the people in society who are the most anxiety-provoking in their behavior.[5] Among the Nupe people of Nigeria, for example, there is much tension between men and their wives. The women, who often have more wealth than the men, frequently engage in trading and shopping expeditions away from their families and express their independence in a number of other ways that run counter to the accepted Nupe standards for virtuous and dutiful women. The analysis shows that ambivalence toward women is at least part of the explanation for the fact that females are much more often accused of witchcraft than are males. Furthermore, the accusations of witchcraft may serve to keep the females somewhat

[4] In *Magic, Science, and Religion* (New York: The Free Press of Glencoe, 1948).

[5] "Witchcraft in Four African Societies," *American Anthropologist*, LIV (1952), 18–29.

under the control of the insecure males, for witchcraft is a serious crime, and steps are taken to punish the alleged offenders.

Guy Swanson has examined a sample of fifty societies in terms of the hypothesis that witchcraft tends to be prevalent when people must interact with one another on important matters in the absence of legitimated social controls and arrangements. He divided his fifty societies into those having important legitimated social controls in most relationships and those in which such controls were lacking, and found a much higher prevalence of witchcraft beliefs in the latter group.

TABLE 3
Relationship of Witchcraft Beliefs
to Presence of Legitimated Social Controls[6]

Prevalence of Witchcraft	Societies Having Legitimated Social Controls	Societies Having Unlegitimated or Uncontrolled Relationships
High	1	17
Intermediate	14	7
Low	9	1

In the language of statisticians, these figures could have occurred simply by chance only 5 times in 10,000. Thus we have strong reasons to believe that there is a relationship between witchcraft and type of social control.

The importance of these findings about magic and witchcraft is greatly increased when we realize that similar phenomena occur in our modern society. Here, however, the "magical" ideas are often translated into twisted beliefs about Communism, fear of fluoridation, scapegoating of minority groups, weird distortions about "what goes on in our universities," and many other puzzling conceptions. From the cross-cultural anthropological evidence as well as from psychological studies, it appears that people who experience fear and frustrations in their daily lives often develop "magical" beliefs about the sources of their problems. They then project the blame onto "witches," who in our modern society may

---

be racial or religious minorities, the government, the politicians, "Communists and other radicals," "those atheists in the university," or other identifiable groups.

As has already been suggested, many of these studies showing strong evidence of the interrelatedness of various human behaviors and beliefs have been produced as a result of the application of psychological principles to analysis of customary behavior.

The study of child training practices by Whiting and Child, which we examined in Chapter 3, is another example of this tendency in anthropological studies. The interaction between anthropological and psychological ideas is a two-way street, however, as is richly illustrated in recent progress in mental health studies.

For example, anthropologists have produced much evidence showing that: (a) mental illness takes different forms in different societies; (b) different societies have different ways of defining what is abnormal behavior; and (c) different peoples have different rates of mental disorder. Some societies in Africa, for example, have very low rates of suicide but have frequent manic outbursts among individuals. On the other hand, certain European societies show a very high suicide and depression rate, with less show of manic outbursts.

Many peoples consider it normal for individuals to experience hallucinations, visions, and trances. Among the people of Bali, for example, several major ceremonies include trance behavior as a regular part of the ritual. The shaman, or medicine man, in many American Indian groups and in Siberia and other parts of the world, regularly gives performances including trance states, hallucinations, and unconsciousness. This behavior among ordinary members of our own society might often lead to a diagnosis of mental instability. However, some small religious sects in American society do regularly become "possessed" and experience trances as part of their religious services. The fact that behavior considered "abnormal" in one society is considered quite "normal" in another raises serious problems for any pan-human concepts of mental health and mental disorder. In this kind of problem, psychiatric and psychological theory has been modified by the cross-cultural findings of the anthropologists. In spite of difficulties in defining what is abnormal or unhealthy personality, most observers are now in agreement that *all* societies have *some* individuals who can be diagnosed clearly as mentally ill, and are so classified by the local people themselves.

Alexander and Dorothea Leighton and their associates have been carrying on an extensive research project in Nova Scotia concerning the relationship between rates of mental illness and types of communities. Their research indicates so far that communities showing relatively greater "social disorganization" have greater numbers of mentally disturbed individuals in the local population.[7] Here, again, anthropological research has amassed evidence for the interrelatedness of community organization, personality characteristics, local customary behavior, religious beliefs, and other elements of peoples' lifeways. Many of the large-scale mental health research projects of recent years have involved close co-operation of anthropologists, psychologists, psychiatrists, and sociologists.

SUMMARY

Anthropology is rather young among established academic studies and cannot claim to have produced extensive and elaborate laws or generalizations about human behavior analogous to the laws and principles of, for example, chemistry, astronomy, or physics. Much of the hundred years or so of anthropological study has been devoted to the very important task of accumulating information—the raw material about human customs and characteristics from which a mature theoretical system can be constructed.

The achievements of anthropology in the collection of discriptive materials have been considerable. Most apparent to the modern educated world is the great mass of information we now have for reconstruction of "what happened in history"—the main outlines of human biological and cultural evolution from simple beginnings over a million years ago. Both human fossil materials and archaeological data supply us with the information for this aspect of anthropological interest.

Ethnographic collections about the great variety of human behavior and customs throughout the world represent another notable achievement of this first descriptive phase of the study of anthropology. Any generalizations about economic systems, religious beliefs, "human nature," etc., can now be built on the foundations of wide-ranging ethnographic information on hundreds of different societies.

---

[7] In *The Character of Danger* (New York: Basic Books, Inc., 1963).

Theoretical developments in anthropology are now beginning to emerge, developed from the accumulated descriptive ethnographies. Refinements in research on cultural evolution have been developed, and a major theoretical structure for understanding the functional organization of human behavior systems is emerging from study of the interrelations of belief systems with elements of social organization and economic arrangements. Many of the important contributions to this growing theoretical system depend on application of psychological concepts and other theoretical ideas borrowed from related social sciences.

Suggested Reading

*Leakey, L. S. B. *Adam's Ancestors.* New York: Harper Torchbooks, 1963.

The discoverer of the very important fossil remains in East Africa writes from a lifetime of research in Old World physical anthropology and archaeology.

*Linton, Ralph. *The Tree of Culture* (abridged). New York: Vintage Books, 1959.

Ralph Linton surveys the culture history and ethnographic data of the major cultural areas of the world in a very readable and interesting way.

*MacGowan, Kenneth, and Joseph A. Hester, Jr. *Early Man in the New World.* ("The Natural History Library"), Garden City: Doubleday and Co., Inc., 1962.

This good-humored account of New World fossil and archaeological remains also includes an excellent introduction to Old World prehistory as background to the arrival of early man in the Americas.

*Spindler, George and Louise (eds.). *Case Studies in Cultural Anthropology.* New York: Holt, Rinehart & Winston, Inc. (series began in 1960).

This series of paperbacks now consists of a number of compact (about 100 pages each), highly readable ethnographic

* Paperback.

accounts of societies such as the Cheyenne, the Tiwi of
Australia, two African native kingdoms (Swazi and Bun-
yoro), a Greek village, a village in India, and Tepoztlan (a
Mexican village). Each culture is described by an anthropologist who carried out field work in that society.

Advanced Reading

*Dobzhansky, Theodosius. *Mankind Evolving*. New Haven and
London: Yale University Press, 1962.

The data on biological evolution, human genetics, and
effects of culture on natural selection are woven together
into an important new view of man's biological present and
future.

*DuBois, Cora. *The People of Alor*. New York: Harper Torchbooks,
1960.

This two-volume work is one of the best available examples
of a "culture-and-personality" study of a society.

*Firth, Raymond. *We the Tikopia*. Boston: Beacon Press, 1963
(first published in 1936).

The Tikopia live on a small, isolated island in the South
Pacific. Raymond Firth, a student of Malinowski and now
one of the most distinguished of British social anthropologists, has described these island people with the same
thoroughness and methodological rigor that his mentor spent
on the Trobriand Islanders.

For the reader who wishes to build a library of anthropological materials, it may be mentioned that a large and rapidly
growing selection of anthropological works is available in paperback editions.

chapter five

Fundamental Insights from Anthropological Research

Many hundreds of thousands of years ago, a "man-ape" sort of creature developed innovations in physical characteristics that made possible a complex speech system, symbolic manipulation of ideas, and much increased storage of information in the brain. Thus man came into being. Through a very gradual evolutionary process, man became increasingly differentiated from the apes and began to shape his lifeways by social traditions, learned behavior, and complex symbolic interaction.

THE CONCEPT OF CULTURE

"Culture" is the word we use to label the "something that was added" that accounts for the large differences in behavior distinguishing man from all the other animals. Culture often means simply the "social heritage" of a given group of people. The social heritage is not a "thing" that is handed down intact, like a hope chest, from generation to generation. It is rather the complex abstraction we could build if it were possible to put together the ideas, patterns of meaning, and "rules" for behavior of all the individuals in a given community. Each new generation reshuffles and changes the systems of ideas, meanings, and rules, so that the social tradition is never fixed and unchanging in any society. Most anthropologists would agree that recognition of the nature and importance of culture is the single most important insight that has marked the development of the study of man.

In studying and comparing cultures both primitive and civilized, we have found that practically all the important differences in lifeways of Americans, Chinese, Australian aborigines, Eskimos, Pygmies of the Congo, and other peoples are understandable as *differences in learned patterns of social behavior,* not differences in biological apparatus, type of brain, type of blood, or any other genetically inherited mechanisms. There is, then, no need to wonder at the idea of "cannibals' sons going to Oxford," as one writer recently put it.

The concept of culture has, of course, become commonly accepted among educated people today, so that it is difficult to realize that only fifty or sixty years ago many scholars still believed the notion that the differences in behavior of Europeans represented different biologically inherited characteristics of the "German race," the "French race," the "English race," and so forth. Recent studies and recent history have demonstrated that individuals from simple cultures, even of "Stone Age culture," become Westernized and adapted to modern culture in incredibly short spans of time; and we are aware that our own Western culture is undergoing rapid change. All of these developments highlight the extremely adaptable nature of human cultural behavior.

POSTULATES OF ANTHROPOLOGY

Our understanding of the general history of science has reached a point where we are well aware that today's accepted fundamental principles are often found tomorrow to be quaint misconceptions of immature scholarship. Therefore, the postulates given below should be looked at critically, with a readiness to discard any or all of them when they have outlived their usefulness. At present, these statements appear to be supported by much available evidence, and they seem to be helpful guides for research and study in anthropology and related subjects.

1. Culture is a total lifeway, not just a superficial set of customs. It largely shapes how man feels, behaves, and perceives as he adapts to his world.

Some earlier scholars took the view that the "customs" of various people are simply a random collection of peculiar beliefs and quaint practices that are a sort of overlay, a more or less colorful glaze, on the outer surface of "natural man." Now we realize that among primitive and civilized peoples alike, our social heritage strongly influences how we perceive and categorize all experience. Even our biological functioning is much shaped by culture. We get hungry at certain times of the day (in different cultures it occurs at different times) because our cultural learning has trained our physiological processes to react at regular "meal times." Our perceptions of sounds, colors, and other "natural" phenomena are conditioned by social experience. Many of the peoples of the world (e.g., the Navaho of the Southwest) do not distinguish between green and blue in their language, apparently because their environments make such distinctions relatively insignificant. On the other hand, Americans lump under the single word *snow* everything from slush to "dry-powdery" in a range of travel conditions that must be carefully distinguished by separate words among the Eskimo, whose lives are greatly influenced by differences in kinds of snow.

Perhaps even more striking is our growing realization that illness is culturally defined and in many ways strongly influenced by cultural patterns. Psychosomatic ailments of all kinds illustrate for us the close interrelations among thoughts, beliefs, and bodily processes. Research in mental health has demonstrated great cultural differences within American society in the interpretation of psychological conditions. In different segments of the American population the same or nearly the same pattern of behavioral characteristics is interpreted in such phrases as "he's psychoneurotic," "he's just acting contrary," "the devil is tempting him," "he is evil," and many other variations.

Culture can kill!—and how different are the situations in various societies that can bring a person to commit suicide. In some societies the jilted lover is the most likely candidate to take his own life; in others it is the recipient of strong criticism from his father. In some societies suicide is so rare that the possible motivations for such an act are little understood by the people.

Well-authenticated cases of "voodoo death" (death by black magic) from various parts of the world provide us with another striking example of the power of cultural belief. It appears that the victim of black magic experiences profound psychophysiological shock when he learns that he has been "attacked" by a sorcerer. He loses appetite for food and water; blood pressure is reduced, blood plasma escapes into the tissues, and the heart deteriorates. He dies of shock that is physiologically the same as "wound shock" in war and highway casualties.

2. *Every cultural system is an interconnected series of ideas and patterns for behavior in which changes in one aspect generally lead to changes in other segments of the system.*

We now have much evidence that in every society the techniques and actions involved in food-getting are closely related to the social organization of the society. For example, most societies in which there is heavy reliance on animal husbandry tend to emphasize the dominance of males, as expressed in inheritance of property through males, and patrilocal choice of residence on marriage. Again, the ethnographic evidence suggests that foraging (hunting and gathering) societies tend to have more lenient child-rearing practices than do agricultural and pastoral peoples. We have noted in the previous chapter how the areas of religious and magical belief appear to be linked to other aspects of social organization.

Studies of changes introduced into primitive societies have demonstrated that it is practically impossible to introduce even the simplest technological innovations without affecting other areas of culture as well. A study of the introduction by missionaries and traders of steel axes into a stone axe-using Australian society showed that far-reaching social changes resulted from this supposedly simple technological change.[1] The stone axes of the traditional culture had been very important, scarce status symbols, owned and controlled by the old men of high prestige and power. The new steel axes upset the entire power system by putting efficient, high-status goods in the hands of women and young men, who had previously occupied subservient positions in the society.

Even games and pastimes, which are often assumed to be trivial, secondary items of behavior, are apparently linked to particular types of social systems. Recent research indicates that practically none of the simpler societies have developed games of strategy. Apparently, societies must have a certain minimum of hierarchical social complexity before problems of strategy become fascinating and entertaining to individuals. Simple hunting and gathering peoples seem to be more attracted to games that capitalize on physical prowess.[2]

---

[1] Lauriston Sharp, "Steel Axes for Stone Age Australians," in *Human Problems in Technological Change*, ed. Edward H. Spicer (New York: Russell Sage Foundation, 1952).
[2] John M. Roberts, Malcolm J. Arth, and Robert R. Bush, "Games in Culture," *American Anthropologist*, LXI (1959), 597–605.

3. Every human cultural system is logical and coherent in its own terms, given the basic assumptions and knowledge available to the given community.

This is mainly a restatement and summary of some points that have already been made, but it deserves repeating in order to lay to rest some earlier ideas that assigned to non-European peoples a "prelogical" or childlike failure to draw appropriate conclusions from experience.

Anthropological field workers have been unable to find any peoples in our world whose systems of reasoning or learning from experience could be called "illogical." The differences in thinking between "primitive man" and "modern man" appear to lie in their fundamental assumptions about the world and things in it, conditioned by differences in available information. Modern man "knows" that the earth revolves around the sun, rather than *vice versa,* because of the complex instruments of observation and calculation that have enabled a very few men in Western civilization to derive a fairly believable theory concerning the solar system. Most primitive peoples are in the position of relying on their eyes alone, according to which it is perfectly reasonable to regard the sun as the moving element, circling the stationary, possibly flat, earth.

Explanations of disease are another familiar area in which modern man has come to have some advantages over non-European thinkers. No primitive man has ever seen a germ. With no "objective" evidence pointing to the physical entities (germs) that have direct causal relationship to illness, primitive man has generally relied on his basic assumption about the universe: the world is full of supernatural spirits and powers which often cause trouble, including illness. If one granted this first premise, it then follows that illness should be treated by means of praying to, cajoling, placating, or driving out the guilty supernaturals. Primitive medical practices therefore make logical sense, granted the fundamental premises. Since most people recover from illness regardless of how they are treated, primitive men have generally had "objective evidence" testifying to the effectiveness of their curing methods.

Concerning mental illness, primitive medicine is even more interesting, for in that area the non-Western medicine man has apparently enjoyed considerable success, and non-Western concepts of therapy have in many areas anticipated modern psychiatric theory. The Iroquois Indians, for example, had in earlier times a winter ceremony in which persons with obsessive dreams and other psychological problems were permitted to act out their compulsions, after their dreams had been interpreted for them by tribal "psychoanalysts."[3] It is instructive to note that primitive medicine men appear to have had, and in some areas still have, therapeutic effectiveness with mental illness that compares favorably with that of modern psychiatry. Such therapeutic effectiveness is not, of course, proof of the correctness of the theories of either group.

Concerning the logic of the "civilized man" versus that of the "primitive," Leopold Pospisil quotes a Papuan native in a "Stone Age" society that was still mainly unaffected by Western culture at the time of his field work in 1955.

> How can you think [asked the native] that a man can sin and can have a free will, and at the same time believe that your God is omnipotent, and that he created the world and determined all the happenings? If he determined all that happens, and [therefore] also the bad deeds, how can a man be held responsible? Why, if he is omnipotent, did the Creator have to change himself into a man and allow himself to be killed [crucified] when it would have been enough for him just to order men to behave?" [4]

The man added that the Christian notion of man resembling God in appearance seemed to him utterly "stupid."

Members of Western society have tended to consider "rationality" in terms of economic self-interest. One branch of Western thinking, economics, has built up an hypothesis of "economic man" as the basis for analysis of important social processes, and many theoreticians have come to think of "economic man" as the model for judgment of human rationality.

It seems that the assumption of "economic man" works relatively well for predicting very gross trends in our own large-scale economy, but it does not appear to be wholly realistic as a yardstick in analysis of many situations in American society. For example, according to assumptions about economically rational man, working people leave areas of unemployment to move to areas of better employment possibilities. Why, then, do not all the economically deprived people of the Appalachian region leave for areas of

---

[3] Anthony F. C. Wallace, "The Institutionalization of Cathartic and Control Strategies in Iroquois Religious Psychotherapy," in *Culture and Mental Disorder*, ed. M. K. Opler (New York: The Macmillan Co., 1959), pp. 63–96.
[4] In *The Kapauku Papuans of West New Guinea* (New York: Holt, Rinehart & Winston, Inc., 1963), p. 85.

better employment possibilities? Again, during periods when there is a relatively saturated labor market in some urban centers of the United States, why do people from some rural areas continue to migrate to these urban centers, where they will have great difficulty in finding employment?

Modern man decides his actions from a very complex array of economic and noneconomic motives, including his emotional attachment to his home and his fear of unknown areas. The economic behavior of non-Western man, too, is based on intelligent seeking of economic advantage, plus a wide array of other, more obscure but understandable motives concerning emotional attachment to home area, loyalty to kinsmen, fear of demands of kinsmen, anxieties about the attitudes of supernatural entities (both his own and white man's gods), and many other motives.

4. The customs and beliefs of peoples are often made more understandable by studying them in terms of the social interrelations among types of individual and group statuses and roles in social action.

Painful ritual circumcision, knocking out of front teeth, other physical "hazing"; the complex of myth-enforced chanting and dancing; assigning of new names to neophytes; and other features of male initiation rites in many societies may seem at first impression senseless and barbaric practices. If they are regarded simply as customs unrelated to other elements of cultural organization, we can derive little understanding of these ceremonies. But these and other sorts of rituals begin to make sense as human acts when we view them as symbolic dramatizations of important status transitions experienced by individuals in the cycle of birth-maturity-death. It remains, then, to examine the particular characteristics of societies with initiation rites to find what special social and psychological characteristics seem especially to account for these ceremonies. One explanation, supported by statistical evidence, finds painful initiation of youths to be related to household arrangements that develop strong cross-sex identification of boys with their mothers.[5] Such household structures are found, for example, in polygynous societies and in societies where married men sleep in "men's houses" while the women and children sleep in their own separate quarters. For boys to become men in such societies, a traumatic "rebirth"

---

[5] John M. Whiting *et al.*, "The Function of Male Initiation Ceremonies at Puberty," in *Readings in Social Psychology*, eds. Maccoby, Newcomb, and Hartley (New York: Holt, Rinehart & Winston, Inc., 1958), pp. 359–70.

accompanied by much symbolizing of new status, is enacted. This kind of analysis of male initiation rites also points to another important general insight that has emerged in the study of anthropology:

5. *The customs and beliefs of peoples are often made more understandable if we examine them from a combined psychological and cultural perspective.*

In addition to the psychological inferences used above in analysis of rituals of status transition, we have noted (in Chapter 4) how beliefs in witchcraft and sorcery are understandable in relation to the anxieties and personality tensions of individuals. Behavior ranging from "mother-in-law avoidance" to complex ceremonies of "ritual rebellion" can be put in clearer perspective by careful interrelating of psychological theory with cultural and social observations. Often this kind of analysis requires use of psychological testing techniques.

6. *Analysis of the implications (or "functions") of cultural behavior must take into account the explicit beliefs and intentions of the people involved; but analysis must also be made of the unnoticed, unintended, further consequences (called "latent functions") of particular acts and beliefs.*

One illuminating example of this principle can be drawn from a look at the custom of binding infants in cradleboards among peoples of the British Columbia coastal area.[6] Among some of these Indians, the custom of binding infants tightly in cradleboards was explained as a beauty measure. It flattened the back of the skulls of infants in a way that was considered handsome by the people. When the custom fell into disuse an important unnoticed latent function of cradleboards was discovered. The cradleboard is a simple baby-tending device! When infants of crawling age were no longer kept in cradleboards, their mothers found themselves with the new task of watching to see that the baby did not crawl into the fire or fall into the nearby water. The Indian mothers did not, therefore, go back to using cradleboards (partly because they are considered "primitive" by Whites), but new patterns of child-tending had to be developed.

---

[6] From Clellan S. Ford as cited by Ward Goodenough in *Cooperation in Change* (New York: Russell Sage Foundation, 1963).

7. Study of practically any behaviors and beliefs among primitive peoples, no matter how unusual, is of direct relevance to understanding our own complex culture, for it appears that humans everywhere shape their beliefs and behavior in response to the same fundamental human problems.

All humans everywhere seek to eat and drink enough, to get shelter from danger and physical discomfort, to secure favorable reactions from their fellows, to be comforted when sick, threatened, or anxious, and to find satisfying explanations for phenomena in the observed world. The solutions to these human problems are of enormous variety, but they all give us clues to the nature of man as a cultural animal.

Human cultural behavior is extremely flexible, so that people have often developed quite different solutions to essentially similar problems. This is a reason why cultures have not all developed through identical, fixed stages of evolution, as the nineteenth-century evolutionists believed. But there is much evidence for the psychic and cultural oneness of mankind:

    a. Striking parallels are found in cultural sequences independently developed in the early civilizations of the Old and the New World. (See pp. 53–56.)

    b. There are a large number of cultural "universals" such as language, kinship systems, modesty concerning natural functions, regulation of sexual behavior, use of fire, naming of individuals, belief in a supernatural world, music and other arts, and dozens of other cultural patterns.

    c. The cross-cultural statistical studies (e.g., as described on pp. 45–47) show correlations among human cultural traits that appear to be based on some sort of psychic unity.

    d. Anthropologists have found no people whose system of language and logic was incomprehensible.

8. Explanation of human behavior is essentially one-sided and incomplete unless information about man's biological, cultural, social, and psychological characteristics is taken into account, together with information about man's biophysical environment.

This fundamental insight provides the rationale for the holistic, integrating style of scholarship that characterizes the study of anthropology.

From the biological side of anthropological studies, these further insights must be added:

9. *Although the peoples of the world may be roughly (and arbitrarily) divided into different "races," or major groups, based on physical characteristics, there are no pure races, and probably never have been. There are large numbers of individuals who are intermediate in racial characteristics, so that no sharp "boundaries" can be drawn separating the "Negroid," "Caucasoid," and "Mongoloid" peoples.*

10. *There is no undisputed evidence of significant differences in ability or intelligence among major racial groupings of the world.*

11. *Contrary to beliefs still widely held, individuals who are the products of racial "mixing," or inter-breeding, are frequently superior to their "pure-blooded" parents in strength, stature, and other characteristics. This phenomenon of "hybrid vigor" is well known among many species of "lower" animals and plants as well.*

12. *Anthropologists (and other scientists) have discovered no human biological characteristics that are unaffected by life experiences and environmental conditions. Conversely, no human characteristics of thought or action can be regarded as unaffected by genetically inherited biological factors.*

Anthropologists have frequently clashed with advocates of "white supremacy," "Aryan superiority," and other forms of racism. Such racists, from Count Gobineau a century ago down to Adolph Hitler and (currently) Carleton Putnam, have either ignored the anthropological evidence altogether or else grossly distorted those materials for their own prejudiced purposes. The central premise of anthropologists in opposition to the racists continues to be:

13. *Practically all the significant differences in behavior among human populations (including expression of attitudes, "intelligence," and other psychological characteristics) are understandable as learned cultural patterns rather than biologically inherited characteristics.*

MAJOR PROBLEMS FOR RESEARCH

Our inventory of the research achievements of anthropology actually represents only a bare initial framework for a science of human behavior. Each of the postulates listed above raises dozens of pertinent research questions. Detailed, precise knowledge that would effectively predict human cultural behavior under particular circumstances is still very far from realization. Anthropologists badly need more precise tools for observing, recording, and analyzing cultures.

A. *Methodological problems for research.*

1. Anthropological observation must be developed to adequately reflect the great variations in behavior found in even the simplest societies. Until recent times anthropologists have paid little attention to problems of "adequate samples" and representativeness of their data. It had been felt that the behavior of primitive people is so bound by custom that there is little variation, so that deviations from custom are readily recognizable. The impression of uniformity of behavior in simple societies is probably a distortion from reality produced by earlier anthropologists' overly simple research techniques and assumptions.

2. New and more culture-free psychological tests and other techniques need to be devised for cross-cultural study of motives, attitudes, values, intelligence, and other individual characteristics. Practically all the tests and devices now used were created for use among literate (often "middle-class") members of Western society, so there are serious problems of comparability of test results even in subgroups within American culture.

3. Anthropological field work must eliminate or at least minimize the effects of the emotional biases of the observer. (One way of partially achieving this goal is through team research, in which several observers with different points of view carry out field work in the same community.)

4. Standard units of observation or behavior that are equally applicable in a wide range of different cultures must be devised. Many of our earlier categories of observation (e.g., patrilocal residence, fertility rites, polytheism, hunting-and-gathering society) are rough-and-ready pigeonholes into which we place a rather mixed bag of actual behavior. More refined concepts are needed in practically all aspects of human behavior.

5. Theoretical constructs such as "acculturation," "individualism," "social disorganization," "cultural disorganization," "co-operation," "male dominance," and many others are badly in need of more refined operational definitions.

6. Anthropologists need to seek out more situations that approximate experimental conditions. For example, anthropologists

can occasionally find pairs (or larger groups) of societies which are culturally very much alike, *except* for some new, "experimental" change in one of the cases, the effects of which the anthropologist can compare with the situation in the society that did not experience the particular introduced change. Modern statistical methods offer the possibility that the anthropologist can observe and measure the differential effects of several variables simultaneously.

7. The relatively simple, face-to-face community study techniques of the anthropologist need to be modified and supplemented for study of complex, multi-community societies, including our own.

B. *Theoretical problems for research.*

As has been suggested above, the theoretical problems crying for research are so numerous that any listing seems pointless or distorted. However, here are some intriguing questions that have frequently haunted anthropologists:

1. To what extent is it possible (and likely) for societies to maintain diversity, even disagreement, on basic values and beliefs and still remain viable, "organized" social systems?

Earlier anthropological (and other social) theory laid great stress on the need for a society to have a consensus of values, or agreement on norms, in order to be healthy. More recently, there has been increasing logical and empirical evidence that such unanimity concerning major values and attitudes is not a *sine qua non* for interaction and cooperation even in simpler social systems.

2. To what extent is it possible (and likely) for peoples to change their beliefs and practices rapidly without suffering cultural disintegration and mental disorder?

Again, the earlier position of anthropologists has been that rapid culture change is inevitably disruptive and unhealthy. All cultures change, however, and most peoples in the world today are experiencing relatively rapid change. The great theoretical problem is: how much and what kinds of changes are "disruptive" and "mentally harmful?"

3. To what extent can similar types of developments in cultural evolution be found among the diverse environments and cultures in the world?

This is the question which the nineteenth-century evolutionists thought they had answered and to which modern anthropologists have now returned with renewed interest. (See discussion of multi-linear evolution in Chapter 4, p. 59.)

4. To what extent, in terms of standards such as mental and physical health, can evaluations be made about some cultural patterns and systems being "better" or "healthier" than others?

Many anthropologists take the view that no absolute judgments can be made concerning the merits of different cultural patterns and systems. On the other hand, those in applied anthropology are engaged in numerous development programs where such cultural evaluations must be made. Billions of dollars are being spent by governments and private agencies in technical assistance, aid to "developing nations," and many other programs that are based on assumptions concerning relative "backwardness," "progress," and other value judgments. The intentions underlying these programs are in most cases quite laudable. But the value judgments involved in the application of these intentions to specific communities are most often left unexamined. Much of the most interesting new knowledge in applied anthropology is in the area of the "unintended consequences" of particular development projects.

Of course, the anthropologist's primary task is not evaluation of cultural patterns as "better" or "worse," for such normative judgments are often the main causes of subjective (and faulty) ethnographic observation. The most important work in anthropology will be in the building of theory in terms of which the varieties of human behavior can become more understandable and predictable. Without such understanding, well-intentioned programs of development and "modernization" can often result in much unintended cultural disorganization and human suffering among the people who are supposed to benefit from such programs.

SUMMARY AND CONCLUSIONS

Man's abilities to create and to manipulate systems of symbolic communication mark him off as distinct from other animals. The various symbol systems—the cultures—of different peoples can all be regarded as ways of adapting to particular environments. Cultural customs must be examined, therefore, in the total context of circumstances in which they occur. We have now accumulated a respectable inventory of cultural descriptions both past and present relating to different environments; an exciting new stage of anthropological study appears to be in the making.

Anthropology is often considered a collection of curious facts, telling about the peculiar appearance of exotic people and describing their strange customs and beliefs. It is looked upon as an entertaining diversion, apparently without bearing upon the conduct of life of civilized communities.

This opinion is mistaken. More than that, I hope to demonstrate that a clear understanding of the principles of anthropology illuminates the social processes of our own times and may show us, if we are ready to listen to its teaching, what to do and what to avoid.[7]

Suggested Reading

Goodenough, Ward. *Cooperation in Change.* New York: Russell Sage Foundation, 1963.

Ward Goodenough, who has made significant contributions to both theoretical and applied anthropology, constructs a systematic framework of anthropological theory for application to programs of planned culture change.

Spicer, Edward A. (ed.). *Human Problems in Technological Change: A Casebook.* New York: Russell Sage Foundation, 1952.

The focus of this casebook is on the cultural reasons for some unexpected problems in programs of technological change: why Eskimos are recalcitrant reindeer herders; why Spanish-Americans rejected an "improved" variety of corn; what happened when some Papago Indians acquired wagons for the first time; and several other interesting cases.

Tax, Sol (ed.). *Horizons of Anthropology.* Chicago: Aldine Publishing Company, 1964.

This collection of papers was prepared for broadcast on a special Voice of America series. The anthropologists chosen for the project represent the younger generation of the discipline (most of them are in their thirties), and their excellent summary articles show that important new theoretical developments are taking place in anthropology.

---

[7] Franz Boas, *Anthropology and Modern Life* (New York: W. W. Norton and Co., 1928).

Index

81